## DATE DUE

INTERLIBRARY LOAN William Jewel
K.C. MO. PUBLIC LIBRARY  MAY 2 1975

# The Untold Story of Panama

## Panama Honors Its Creators

WALDORF-ASTORIA
New York, February 20th, 1941

# The Untold Story of Panama

### Panama Honors Its Creators

A rare document: Souvenir of luncheon given by Dr. Amador's son Raoul on his father's Inauguration Day to honor the men who, they said, did most to make possible the "independence" of Panama.

Dr. MANUEL AMADOR
First President of the Republic of Panama

## LUNCHEON

Tendered by

Dr. R. A. Amador

To

| | |
|---|---|
| WILLIAM NELSON CROMWELL | E A DRAKE |
| GEO H. SULLIVAN | CHARLES PAINE |
| E. B. HILL | R L. WALKER |
| WILLIAM J. CURTIS | S DEMING |
| R. L. FARNHAM | Dr. M. J. ECHEVERRIA |

*WALDORF - ASTORIA*
*New York, February 20th, 1904*

Cromwell as he appeared in June, 1911, from a photograph in THE METROPOLITAN MAGAZINE, illustrating an article by M. E. Stone, Jr., "Theodore Roosevelt - Please Answer"

Raoul Amador shortly before his death in Paris - 1934, and one of several letters to Earl Harding showing Amador's cooperation in 1909-10.

(translation from Amador's Spanish)

October 18, 1903

Dear Little Son:

I received your telegram that you are not coming, as they have refused you permission.

Also received your letter of the 17th. If the wreath does not come, they will send it from the *Endicott by the next steamer.

The reason for your coming was for you to meet Bunau-Varilla, to whom I have spoken of you. He said that if all turns out well, you shall have a good place on the medical commission, which is the first that will begin work; that my name is in Hay's office and that certainly nothing will be refused you.

The plan seems to me good. A portion of the Isthmus declares itself independent and that portion the United States will not allow any Colombian forces to attack.

An Assembly is called, and this gives authority to a Minister to be appointed by the new Government in order to make a treaty without need of ratification by that Assembly.

The treaty being approved by both parties, the new Republic remains under the protection of the United States, and to it are added the other districts of the Isthmus which do not already form part of the new Republic, and these also remain under the protection of the United States.

The movement will be delayed a few days--we want to have here the Minister who is going to be named so that once the movement is made he can be appointed by cable and take up the treaty. In 30 days everything will be concluded.

We have some resources on the movement being made, and already this has been arranged with a bank.

As soon as everything is arranged I will tell B.-V. to look out for you. He says if you do not wish to go he will look out for a position for you in New York. He is a man of great influence.

A thousand embraces to Pepe and my remembrances to **Jenny and Mr. Smith.

Your affectionate father,<br>AMADOR

P. S. - I leave two parcels at Annie's. I did not send them as it will be no use to have you bring them back with you. Adios.

* Hotel Endicott, New York, was Dr. Amador's headquarters.
** Jenny A. Smith was the American wife of Dr. Amador's son Raoul.

MEMORANDUM OF AGREEMENT

WHEREAS, J. P. Morgan & Co, J. Edward Simmons, James Stillman, Isaac Seligman, Douglas Robinson, Henry W. Taft, H. H. Rogers, J. P. Delamar and others, desire to purchase certain shares of the capital stock of the Compagnie Nouvelle Du Canal de Panama Company, at such terms, and upon such conditions as may be named by a committee of three persons to be selected from the parties to this agreement;

NOW, THEREFORE, we, the undersigned, for ourselves, our administrators and assigns, in consideration of the mutuality hereof, have agreed to and with each other as follows:

First: To purchase as many shares of the capital stock of the Compagine Nouvelle Du Canal de Panama Company as possible, at a price not exceeding twenty per cent (20%) per share, per par value of One Hundred Dollars ($100.)

Second. When so acquired, to place the whole of said shares of stock in the hands of the committee herein before refered to.

Third: Said stock is to be held by said committee for the benefit of the parties to this agreement, and to be disposed of at a price not less than Fifty-five (55%) per share on a basis of One Hundred Dollars ($100) par value.

The proceeds of the sale of the stock, after deducting all and any expenses in acquiring and in making the sale thereof, are to be devied pro rata among the parties to this agreement, and according to the respective amount subscribed and paid in by them for the purchase of the aforementioned stock.

IN WITNESS WHEREOF, the parties hereto have set their hands and seals this Twenty-Fifth day of May Ninteen hundred ( May 25, 1900)

In the presence of.

MR. ISAAC N. SELIGMAN,

In Account With  J & W. SELIGMAN & CO.

```
1902
Aug. 6  To 1500 Panama Canal 6% 1st Series, Separate A/c )
 "   "   "  1000    "      "   6%  2nd    "       "    " )   $ 34,384.75
Oct.13  "    881    "      "   6%  1st    "       "    " )
 "   "  "    619    "      "   6%  2nd    "       "    " )     30,129.50
Nov.30  "   1475    "      "   6%  1st    "    Special A/c     23,543 26
Dec. 5  "    125    "      "   New Stock,   "       "           2,533.14
1904
Jan.11  "    175    "      "   6% 1st Series,  "    " )
 "   "  "    177    "      "   6% 2nd     "    "   " )
 "   "  "    174    "      "   5%         "    "   " )
 "   "  "    194    "      "   4%         "    "   " )
 "   "  "    150    "      "   3%         "    "   " )         11,021.74
 " 13   "    917    "      "   New Stock,  "       "           20,064 16
Apr.11  "   1000    "      "    "    "     "       "           23,942 95
Jun.29  "  Delivered in Paris by Mr Kahn on instructions )
              given by Paul M. Warburg for a/c of Isaac )
              " S :                                     )
              328 Panama Canal 6% 1st Series            )
              146    "      "   6%  2nd    "           )
              458    "      "   5%         "           )         ----
              374    "      "   4%         "           )
              355    "      "   3%         "           )
              203    "      "   Lottery Bonds          )
               60    "      "   New Stock              )
1905
Sep.20  "  Received from the Liquidator in Paris )
              815 Panama Canal Lottery Bonds    )  Spec'l A/c
 "   "  "  1353 Panama Can.Lott.Bds , Separate A/c
 "   "  "    475   "     "     "     "    A/c Warburg
 "   "  "     20   "     "     "     "    A/c Coupons
 "  29  "     11 6417  "   "     "     "    Bought of Jefferson S.  255.34
 "   "  "   802-4440  "    "     "     "    Bought of J & W S.& Co  17,599 50
Oct.17  "  his proportion of Paris Joint A/c)
              145 20 Panama Canal Lott Bds. )                   2,946 09
 "   "  "    2 70   "     "     "    "    Bought of Isaac S.
                                               London             54 78
1903
Oct.13  "  2000 Panama Canal New Stock, Special A/c           27,020.51
May 20  "  1250    "      "    "    "    Separate             25,972.15
Aug.13  "  fos.11,000 50 abandoned call Panama Stk.,Separate   2,125.70
1905
Oct.25  "    "  11,000 B.F Winslow, Special A/c                2,130.09
```

PAUL M. WARBURG

```
1903
May 20  To 1250 Panama Canal New Stock              25,965.64
             Cables                                     12.00

1904
Feb.15  By 850 Panama Canal New Stock               18,748 78
Mch. 9   "  400    "      "    "    "                8,854 97
```

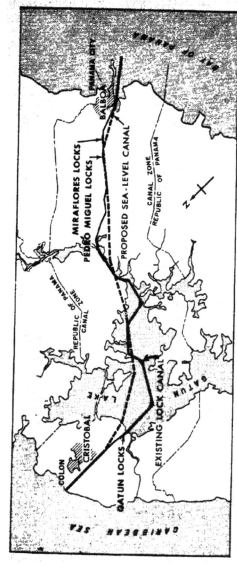

SEA-LEVEL PLAN showing approximate course in relationship to present canal

THE DOTTED LINE INDICATES SEA-LEVEL CANAL SUGGESTED IN 1947. IT WOULD REQUIRE A NEW TREATY, SINCE CANAL ZONE LIMITS WOULD BE CHANGED. PANAMA COULD EXACT ANY PRICE.

October, 1913   The WORLD'S WORK   Pages 674-680

# IN JUSTICE TO COLOMBIA

HOW TO SETTLE THE DISPUTE WHICH AROSE WHEN WE "TOOK" PANAMA — THE WIDE IMPORTANCE OF THE PROBLEM IN SOUTH AMERICA — FOR A WIDER CANAL ZONE

BY

EARL HARDING

[*The author of this article went to the Isthmus of Panama and to Bogota in 1909 and 1910 to dig out the hidden history of the Panama secession  In this way he was brought in contact with the Colombian people more intimately perhaps than any foreigner could be who had not his special mission   The result of his two-years' study of the Panama question was presented to the Foreign Affairs Committee of the House of Representatives under the Rainey Resolution to investigate the 'taking' of Panama* — THE EDITORS]

\* \* \* \* \* \* \* \* \* \* \*

THE CANAL AND ITS SURROUNDINGS
SHOWING THE WIDTH OF THE CANAL ZONE IF IT INCLUDED COLON AND PANAMA AND THE WATERSHED OF THE CHAGRES RIVER  AND SHOWING THE TERRITORY EAST OF THE CANAL THAT MIGHT BE GIVEN BACK TO COLOMBIA

THE PROBLEMS OF DUAL SOVEREIGNTY ARE NOT NEW - the author outlined them in 1913 in the above article and accompanying illustration.

EARL HARDING IS GREETED BY THE PRESS.

ONE ALTERNATIVE TO MONOPOLY

# THE UNTOLD STORY OF PANAMA

New York Journal on Nov 19, 1901.

EARL HARDING

# The Untold Story
# of
# Panama

## by *Earl Harding*

ATHENE PRESS, INC
252 LEXINGTON AVENUE
NEW YORK 16, N Y

The Untold Story of Panama

Copyright 1959 by Earl Harding
Printed in the United States of America

All rights in this book are reserved

No part of this book may be used or reproduced in any manner whatsoever without written permission except in the case of brief quotations embodied in critical articles and reviews. For information address Athene Press Inc., 252 Lexington Avenue, New York 16, N. Y.

Distributed by

THE BOOKMAILER, Inc
Box 101, Murray Hill Station
New York 16, N. Y.

To the Memory of

Joseph Pulitzer, Frank Irving Cobb, Don C. Seitz
Robert Hunt Lyman Caleb M. Van Hamm and my other
associates on *The World*, and Delavan Smith,
Charles R. Williams and Hilton U. Brown
of *The Indianapolis News*,
who fought and won the battle
for Freedom of the Press
and laid the foundations for this book

and
with abiding love and appreciation

To my wife
Louise Graham Harding
Member American Society of International Law
and International Bar Association
for her counsel and inspiration
in writing The Untold Story

# THE UNTOLD
# STORY OF PANAMA

## *Paid by United States Taxpayers*

1904 — To bondholders of defunct "Old" Panama Canal Company and to stockholders of bankrupt "New" French company — or to speculators who had gambled in the French securities     $40,000,000
(For his forty millions Uncle Sam was to get the rusty digging equipment of the French, the Panama Railroad which the French had purchased, their about-to-lapse concession from Colombia, and the French companies' "archives" — which were never delivered )

1904 — To the Republic of Panama, creature of U S.-protected "revolution" of 1903     10,000,000

1922 — To Colombia, in partial reparation for T R 's having "taken" the Isthmus     25,000,000

To Panama in annuities     20,500,000
    1913 to 1933, 21 payments at $250,000
    1934 to 1955, 22 payments at 430,000
    1956-57-58, 3 payments at 1,930,000

          ° $95,500,000

° This total does not include $24,300,000 "fair market value" of Canal Zone properties given to Panama by the 1955 treaty, nor the cross-Canal bridge to cost the United States upward of $20,000,000, nor the million-plus paid to Panama for "rental" of defense sites during World War II, nor the U S Government's total investment in the Canal enterprise, as of June 30, 1953, audited by the Comptroller General as $489,162,524, nor the many more millions spent on maintenance and operation of the Panama Canal.

## *Author's Preface*

United States citizens have on their hands a continuing struggle to keep control of the lifeline of their national defense and the backbone of their ocean commerce — the United States-built and United States-owned Panama Canal

Nasser set a pattern for canal seizure at Suez in 1956. Although legally inapplicable to the Panama Canal, the Nasser example of expropriation delighted Panamanian radicals The danger implicit in ignoring their reactions was not recognized by most North Americans, who have assumed for half a century that trouble at Panama always evaporates.

Seriousness of the situation at the Isthmus was brought home to the United States by the Nixon incidents in Lima and Caracas in May, 1958 and by almost coincident outbreaks of wild disorder in Panama, with defiant challenging of United States sovereignty over the Canal Zone, preceded by a Panamanian flag-planting "invasion" of the Zone heralded to the world as "Operation Sovereignty."

Pressures little realized by the North American public have been building up steadily and persistently in Panama and elsewhere ever since the Suez crisis, with these objectives

1. *Nationalization* of the Panama Canal by the Republic of Panama — an avowed permanent aspiration of Panamanian youth Pending nationalization, to reassert Panama's claim to sovereignty over the Canal Zone and the "right" to fly Panamanian flags there, to require the United States to establish Spanish as the official language in the Zone, and at the same time to demand more and still more "benefits" for Panama under United States treaties — all with strong backing of high Panamanian officials and much of the Panamanian press

2. *Annulment* of Panama's 1903 treaty grant of sovereign control of the Canal Zone to the United States "in perpetuity" as allegedly "contrary to international law"

3. *Internationalization* of the Panama Canal under control of the United Nations

4. *Expropriation*, in effect, by demanding for Panama at least 50/50 division of *gross* income from Canal tolls (in 1958 the *gross* was $42,834,006 and the *net* to the United States was $2,656,382) — or another vast increase in United States annuity payment, which started at $250,000, went to $430,000 and at this writing is $1,930,000

Still another threat of eventual expropriation is in Panama's December, 1958 law extending the Republic's coastal waters to a 12-mile limit This law was passed with representations that it will enable Panama to close the seaward ends of the United States Canal Zone, compel all ships using the Canal to fly the Panama flag, to recognize Panama's sovereignty, and to pay whatever taxes Panama may levy on such shipping, and, if necessary, have this issue adjudicated in an international court

To this complex of political problems has been added since World War II a tangle of economic, engineering and defense questions:

1. Should the capacity of the present high-level lake-and-locks system of the Panama Canal be expanded to meet present and future needs? Such expansion, already overdue, is possible under present treaties with Panama and at relatively moderate cost.
2. Would conversion to a sea-level strait make the Panama Canal enough safer from atomic destruction to justify a cost of unforeseeable billions of dollars plus diplomatic uncertainties and unfathomable hazards from rock slides? Change to sea-level, because it would make some changes in Canal Zone boundaries, would require a new treaty — for which Panamanian politicians could exact any price.
3. Should the United States in the light of recent experiences, anticipate that Panamanian demands may become so unreasonable that another canal should be planned now? The United States still holds, under the Bryan-Chamorro Treaty of August 5, 1914, "exclusive proprietary rights" in perpetuity for the "construction, operation and maintenance" of a canal through Nicaragua

As Representative Daniel J Flood of Pennsylvania told Congress, on May 29, 1957, the United States in successive treaty revisions beginning in 1936-39 threw away its bargaining power with Panamanian politicians. Sorely needed on both sides of the bargaining table will be North Americans and Panamanians who know, and will squarely face, the cold, hard facts of history.

Anti-American attitudes in Panama can be traced directly to the fact that Panamanians of the present generation have never been told the whole truth — how, and why, and by whom their little Republic was created. A great many

North Americans are almost as uninformed. A realistic reappraisal of the history of United States relations with the Republic of Panama is essential to a better understanding. For, without knowledge of that history, neither North Americans nor Panamanians can reach sound and just conclusions as to their rights, responsibilities and obligations when the recurring problems of the Isthmian area demand solution

o o o

Building of the Panama Canal required leadership and financing by the United States. President Theodore Roosevelt considered it the greatest achievement of his administration, as important for the United States as was the Louisiana Purchase in 1803 The disruptive proposals now advanced for making over the relationships at Panama — some of them of communist origin — might be classed with a suggestion that the Louisiana Purchase be rescinded!

The leaders who wrought the world-important enterprise at Panama have passed on without telling all of the story. Succeeding generations, in Panama as well as in the United States, have lost sight of or never knew essential facts bearing on the history of that great undertaking Facts that belong to history are disclosed for the first time in this book

Controversy over the creation of the Republic of Panama in 1903 came to a climax when President Theodore Roosevelt in 1908 demanded that Joseph Pulitzer, owner of the *New York World*, two of his editors, and two publishers of the *Indianapolis News* be prosecuted for alleged criminal libel for what they had published about the "Panama scandal." A *cause celebre* comparable in importance for a free press to the famous defense of John Peter Zenger two centuries earlier resulted, after two years, in a sweeping defeat of the Rooseveltian charges in the United States Supreme Court, on questions of law.

Meanwhile, the Pulitzer defense on questions of fact had to be assembled for presentation in court if the prosecution

*Authors Preface* v

went that far — which it never did. I had been in the Pulitzer organization only four years and had just been made Day News Editor of the Morning World when I was asked to take charge of an intensive investigation of the antecedents of the Panama Republic I was told that it might require two or three months. It took all of my waking hours for more than two years. Being then 10 to 15 years the junior of *The World's* editors and lawyers who took an active part throughout that two-years' legal struggle, I am the sole survivor

It happened that I learned early the value of preserving records, so, long after I moved from journalism into the business world I put in fireproof storage documented facts about the history of the Panama "revolution" of 1903 which could not be disclosed even when much of the evidence which I developed in 1909 and 1910 was presented to a committee of Congress in 1912. Many obscure gaps in Isthmian history can now be filled in.

The Panama Canal is a tremendous service to the free world, and especially to our Latin-American neighbors. Its continued efficient operation is indispensable to their wellbeing. The mounting crises since 1956 demand that the whole story of Panama be told.

New York, February 11, 1959

*Earl Harding*

## Contents

|  | Page |
|---|---|
| *Author's Preface* | I-V |

Threats of nationalization, annulment of 1903 treaty, internationalization under UN, and expropriation by Panama are the reasons for writing The Untold Story.

*Antecedents of the Panama Canal*     1

U S. committed to Nicaragua route when French started and failed at Panama. They retain William Nelson Cromwell and he changed history. New crises demand re-evaluation of rights and responsibilities.

*"Napoleonic Strategy" Applied to Panama*     7

Pressagents and lobbyists manipulate Congress and public opinion. Investigations by Walker Commissions. How Lewis M. Haupt was "persuaded." Cromwell's hand in ultimatum to Colombia.

***Pre-Natal Labor in the Birth of a Republic***     23
    Panama Railroad men, responsible to Cromwell, were major factor. "Planned alibis." Amador's resolute wife saved the "revolution."

***The Baby Republic Is Born***     38
    Bunau-Varilla's versions. Efforts by Amador, Boyd and Cromwell to have him removed First flag of Panama given to the White House

***Theodore Roosevelt Challenges a Free Press***     47
    Inside story of origin of T. R.'s libel prosecution of New York and Indianapolis publishers and his first defeat by historic decision of Judge Anderson.

***Who Really Got the American Taxpayers' $40,000,000***     55
    How evidence of syndicate agreement and proof of speculation in French Panama Canal securities (denied by T. R.) came to Pulitzer's *World*, and why never published until now. How evidence was run down in Paris.

***Amador's "Dear Little Son" Held History's Key***     69
    Panama patriots' contradictory testimony refuted by telltale letter. How it was obtained, and why it escaped destruction.

***Panamanians Learn Early the Art of Political Blackmail***     76
    They shook down T. R. in 1908 and taught their sons how to get what they want from Uncle Sam.

***Amador Got His Assurance Direct From T. R.***     83
    He would not trust Cromwell's nor Bunau-Varilla's promises but went himself at night to White House, as Senator Morgan heard

***Coverups and Contradictions***     89
    Early accountings burned in Panama. Bunau-Varilla's varying tales. His attacks on Cromwell. Financing of the "revolution" still shrouded.

**Contents** ix

*At Long Last T. R. Has "Nothing to Say!"* 96
How the invincible Roosevelt took the bitter news of unanimous Supreme Court decision killing his libel prosecution of publishers.

*Dual Sovereignty Breeds Perpetual Discord* 101
Need for wider Canal Zone to include terminal cities pointed out by this author in 1913. U. S. rights sacrificed in first giveaway treaty of 1936. New claims of "sovereignty" over Canal Zone. Spruille Braden's experienced warning ignored

*1955 Giveaway Treaty Jammed Through;*
*"Mutual Consent" Is Only Way Out* 113
Treaty secretly negotiated, inadequately considered by U. S Senate Panamanian politicians demand still more

*Just Who Are Behind the Drives to*
*Internationalize and to Nationalize* 119
Harry S. Truman, James P. Warburg. Senator Flanders, James Roosevelt, Clement Atlee, Hugh Gaitskell, *The Methodist Reporter*, Panamanian Student Federation, communists, "liberal" professors and politicians.

*Isthmian Uproar Redoubled* 130
Alger Hiss' telling UN that Canal Zone is "Occupied Territory" launches proclamations of Panama's "sovereignty" over Canal Zone and demands for nationalization of Canal by Panama. Affronts to the Milton Eisenhower mission.

*"Operation Sovereignty"* 137
Panamanian flag-planting in Canal Zone, prolonged bloody riots, demands for 50/50 division of *gross*, not *net*, revenue of Canal enterprise mark critical year 1958. Representative Flood gives Congress a record of unstable government in Panama.

*The Heritage of Conflict* 146
   History of Panama Republic clouded by contradictory claims of Cromwell and Bunau-Varilla. Keynote of $25,000,000 settlement with Colombia.
*Navigable Lake Canal vs. Sea-Level at Panama* 151
   Reorganization by Congress. Makeshift and Squandermania. Would sea-level at Panama be safer? New Board of Consultants merits taxpayers' confidence. Modernization at Panama and possible alternatives under consideration.
*Nicaragua — Alternative to Monopoly at Panama* 165
   Bryan-Chamorro Treaty of 1914 cost U. S. $3,000,000. Its terms and provisions
*Recommended Reading* 172
*Index* 174

*Chapter 1*

# Antecedents of the Panama Canal

Readers of schoolbook histories know that the opening of the Panama Canal in 1914 was the fruition of four centuries of searching for ways and means to link the Atlantic and Pacific Oceans But the vital importance to the United States, to Latin America and to the world is not today so generally realized as it was when the Canal was completed.

Beginning with Balboa's first sight of the Pacific from the heights of Panama in 1513, every possible crossing of the land-strip between the oceans was explored Eventually two routes were found most practicable for a ship canal — Nicaragua and Panama

Details of the adventures and misadventures of canal searchers have filled volumes of histories We shall concern ourselves here with a tightly condensed summary of events leading up to the Panama Canal and the early — and perhaps not yet ended — competition between the routes of Panama and Nicaragua

o o o

Primitive transit facilities across Panama and through Nicaragua by river and lake boats and connecting stagecoaches were served for many years by coastwise ships from New York and San Francisco. High transit dues collected at Panama led men of broader vision to look elsewhere. The distance between New York and San Francisco via Nicaragua, some 400 miles shorter than via Panama, was one incentive. Then the Mexican war, 1846, further emphasized the need for coast-to-coast transit, which railroads did not provide even in a limited way until 1869. So in 1849 Cornelius Vanderbilt and associates organized the American Atlantic and Pacific Ship Canal Company and made the first comprehensive survey for a canal via Lake Nicaragua.

Good relations with Nicaragua and the use of its primitive transit facilities were paralyzed by the filibustering expeditions of an American adventurer, William Walker, and the Vanderbilt concession was canceled in 1856.

Meanwhile the United States by its 1846-48 treaty with New Granada (later re-named Colombia) was getting relief from discriminatory transit dues and civil disturbances in Panama. In return, the United States guaranteed neutrality on the Isthmus and New Granada's "rights of sovereignty and property" in its province or Department of Panama.

This stabilizing treaty hastened construction of the Panama Railroad across the Isthmus by private American capital. This first transcontinental railroad was chartered by the New York State legislature in April, 1849. The incorporators were New York businessmen and financiers, John L. Stephens, William H Aspinwall, President of the Pacific Mail Steamship Company, and Henry Chauncey, prominent New York capitalist.

Opened for traffic in 1855, the Panama Railroad enjoyed a near-monopoly until an investigating commission, appointed by President Grant in 1872, reported unanimously in 1876 that Nicaragua would be the preferable canal route. Panama, because of climatic and geologic conditions, was considered undesirable if not impossible. President Hayes, following President Grant's initiative, sent a special message to Congress, March 8, 1880, announcing. "The policy of this country is a canal under American control."

While United States interest was centering on possibilities of a canal through Nicaragua, the French, inspired by their success at Suez in 1869, obtained in 1878 a concession from New Granada to build through Panama This spurred the United States to get rid of the impediment to single-control of a canal, to which it had agreed with Great Britain in 1850 The Hay-Pauncefote Treaty of 1901 removed that obstacle.

In the three decades since President Grant named the first canal commission, public opinion and governmental policy in the United States had coalesced in favor of an all-American canal through Nicaragua. The United States Congress chartered the Maritime Canal Company of Nicaragua, May 9, 1889 and former Senator Warner Miller of New York, as president, started work with a subsidiary Nicaragua Canal Construction Company. The panic of 1893 dried up the flow of funds and left the Nicaragua canal enterprise in receivership.

Then came the war with Spain The need for a canal was made still more obvious by the voyage of the *Oregon* around South America to join the United States fleet off Santiago. Public sentiment for a canal became clamorous. Friends of the Nicaragua project turned to the government for help. Bills for a Nicaragua canal were passed by both Senate and House, but mysterious influences held up the Senate bill in the House or the House bill in the Senate. Lobbyists of the then new and prosperous transcontinental railroads were credited with killing unwanted maritime competition.

* * *

But other influences, equally mysterious for many years, were boring from within and without. The Panama Railroad, which had cost its American builders about $5,000,000, was essential for canal building by the French.

Through the influences of an American syndicate the Panama Railroad was sold to the Panama Canal Company of France for something over $20,000,000 The price seemed extortionate to the French, but they were helpless It took about one-third of the French company's capital and contributed to its eventual bankruptcy.

Mismanagement, extravagance and graft, compounding an initial error in planning, brought suspension in 1889 of canal digging at Panama begun by the French February 1, 1881 To escape imprisonment in France for fraud and to salvage some part of their huge investment, the "penalized stockholders" of the first, commonly called the Old Panama Canal Company, organized in 1894 the New Panama Canal Company Work at Panama was resumed, and was continued sporadically in order to keep alive the concession from Colombia and retain the canal company's title to its profitable Panama Railroad But the new company was inadequately financed and its concession, which had been extended by the Colombian government by executive rather than by legislative action, would soon expire The outlook seemed hopeless, since the United States was committed to building the rival canal through Nicaragua

The French knew something of the capacity of a New York lawyer who had been a director and general counsel of the Panama Railroad since 1893 Ready to grasp any helping hand, the staggering Frenchmen retained him — William Nelson Cromwell — as their American attorney, January, 1896. They retained him in the belief that he could divert the United States from Nicaragua to Panama, guide them in obtaining more capital, and eventually assist them in unloading on United States taxpayers the French equipment on the Isthmus and their about-to-lapse Colombian concession

Cromwell was successful — so much so that he billed his French clients for $832,449.38 for fees and disbursements allegedly still due him up to December 23, 1907. In a bill of particulars or brief to support his claim, Cromwell said

*Antecedents of the Panama Canal* 5

his services had "involved almost every branch of professional activity — engineering, law, legislation, finance, diplomacy, administration and direction" — so extensive that "it would be altogether impossible to give details, even if it were proper to do so."

Some of the long-hidden details of Cromwell's services are an essential part of history which every United States citizen and every Panamanian should know when their respective rights and responsibilities are at issue and questions such as these demand truthful answers.

Did William Nelson Cromwell plan and promote and in part finance the Panama "revolution" of 1903 — or who did? Was Cromwell the real father of the little Republic or was he only midwife at its birth? Or did the Frenchman Philippe Bunau-Varilla perform part or all of these functions? Did either Cromwell or Bunau-Varilla in their voluminous writings and testimony tell the whole truth?

Who got *all* of the American taxpayers' $40,000,000 which allegedly was paid in full to the French for their bankrupt property? Or did a speculating syndicate of United States financiers and politicians get a big share?

What interests and influences are behind the persistent campaigns for Panama to nationalize and for the United Nations to internationalize the Canal? United States taxpayers had a net investment in the Canal close to half a billion uninflated dollars when a reorganization audit was made by the Comptroller General of their government in 1952. What will happen to their investment and eventually to their freedom if the lifeline of their national defense is lost?

And how can American citizens who love their own country be alerted in time to these dangers, which are so much nearer to them than are the dangers in the Middle or Far East?

Fortunately some have been alerted — notably a few members of the United States Senate and House of Representatives; and among citizen groups the **Daughters of the**

American Revolution, who have sounded an alarm to their member chapters. Also thousands of readers of *The Christian Science Monitor* are aware, because the courageous and far-seeing correspondent of *The Monitor* in the Canal Zone, Ralph Skinner, has given that great newspaper more of the facts than press services have supplied their readers about the anti-American agitation that has been boiling in Panama ever since the Suez crisis of 1956.

Readers of *The Saturday Evening Post* of October 25, 1958 were alerted by a strong editorial, "The U. S. A. Can't Surrender Its Rights in the Panama Canal." Syndicated columnists Edward Tomlinson, Constantine Brown and Ruth Montgomery have given their readers some of the disquieting developments, but generally North American editors seem to have assumed that public interest did not focus on Isthmian problems.

Most alert of all has been the American Legion, nationally and through its Canal Zone branch, known as its Department of the Panama Canal. The *Legion Magazine* warned its readers in March, 1957 in bold headlines. "Let's Look at Our Own Canal; We May Lose It, Thanks to the Internationalists!" The *Legion Magazine's* writer, Maurice Ries, a veteran fighter against communism, summarized:

"The Panama Canal is our jugular vein, our lifeline. Cut it and the United States dies Wrest it from our control and in matters of seaborne commerce and naval defense the U. S east and west coasts again become, as once they were, months instead of days apart

"Block it and our foreign commerce strangles. Take it away from us and we have no further right to establish defenses so far to the south.

"The result will be that then our hemispheric relations will change, and our foreign policy must change, and no man on earth can say what might happen to this nation once that chain reaction is set in motion."

*Chapter 2*

# "Napoleonic Strategy" Applied to Panama

Intimate details of the story of Panama would still be sealed behind iron curtains of disputed and distorted history if William Nelson Cromwell had not made the greatest miscalculation of his astounding career. Had he kept his nerve and remained silent instead of complaining to a public prosecutor against alleged "blackmailers," the Theodore Roosevelt prosecution of Joseph Pulitzer for alleged criminal libel would never have been initiated, and some individual, to this day unidentified, would have lacked incentive to plant secretly on the desk of a Pulitzer editor a copy of Cromwell's telltale brief or bill of particulars which revealed his hand in creating the Republic of Panama.

What history will always remember as the Panama scandal simmered into public prints at the time of the "revolution" of 1903. Intermittently it bubbled out of Congressional inquiries lasting into 1906; but it did not boil over until

President Theodore Roosevelt fired it with his explosive language in 1908. Senator John T. Morgan of Alabama, supporter of a United States canal through Nicaragua, had fought with only partial success to expose what he believed to have been the illegal and immoral part of the United States in dismembering Colombia and setting up Colombia's Department of Panama as the Republic of Panama.

Pitiless publicity at times deepened public suspicion, but Senator Morgan could never pin down the evasive and defiant Cromwell. Today equivalent conduct of a witness before a Congressional committee would most likely bring citations for contempt. But influences bent on covering up the Panama scandal were so powerful that Cromwell could, and did, plead the privilege of a lawyer to protect the secrets of his client as glibly and successfully as subversives now take the Fifth Amendment.

Cromwell told his French clients soon after he accepted their retainer as general counsel in January, 1896 that "no one in the United States doubted that the Panama Canal in itself was an impossibility. Public opinion demanded the Nicaragua Canal." He concentrated his early lobbying on defeating Nicaragua bills in Senate and House. By 1897 he projected "a vigorous policy of publicity, enlightenment and opposition," and in 1898 created a special press bureau for anti-Nicaragua and pro-Panama propaganda. "We must," he told his French clients, "make our plans with Napoleonic strategy."

Recruited for the Cromwell press bureau were Roger L. Farnham and Jonas M. Whitley. Both had won their journalistic spurs on the Wall Street staff of Joseph Pulitzer's *World* and were well equipped. Farnham, as press bureau chief, also doubled as adjunct to the several members of the Cromwell law firm who spent weeks on end in Washington enlightening members of Senate and House and Administration officials.

Cromwell's "Napoleonic strategy" was never fully described until he filed with French arbitrators, September 5,

1907, a 65,000-word brief to support his claim that the French Panama Canal Company still owed his firm $832,449.38 for fees and disbursements In their own words, quoted from the brief, this is how the Cromwell lobby started the propaganda that continued long after the Panama Republic was born.

"We write an elaborate pamphlet containing a full exposition of the Panama Canal and circulate it in Congress, throughout the press, and among all the influential classes in the United States."

"We obtain a public hearing before the Committee of the House and make a full exposition."

"We obtain the passage, March 3, 1899, of a bill appointing a new Commission to examine the Panama and other canal routes, and by this means we prevent the final passage of the Nicaragua canal bills."

Not content with getting a breathing-spell for his French clients by creation of a new Commission, Cromwell undertook to guide the selection of its personnel President McKinley disregarded Cromwell's list of acceptable experts and on June 9, 1899, appointed to this, the second Walker Commission, three members of the first Walker Commission who had reported in favor of Nicaragua They were Rear Admiral John G Walker, Colonel Peter C. Hains, U.S A, and Lewis M Haupt Supplementing them were eight appointees who had had experience with Isthmian transit problems

Cromwell then "laid aside all his other business" and during the six months following the appointment of the second Walker Commission "devoted himself exclusively to the official presentation of the Panama matter to the Commission so as to convince it of the superiority of this route." He "urged the Commission to go to Paris in a body" — instead of going first to Panama and Nicaragua — and himself sailed for Paris on August 5, 1899, ahead of the Commission "to prepare and direct the presentation" of his case for the Panama route.

The Walker Commission's sessions in Paris continued into September, but Cromwell remained through October and "held absorbing daily conferences" on Company business, including "the formation of syndicates" and on "Americanization of the canal, an idea of our own."

Cromwell returned to New York November 1, 1899 with power of attorney from the French company to carry out his plan of "Americanization." He soon found that "to interest important capitalists in the United States in such an enterprise was an undertaking so arduous as to seem really impossible." Nevertheless, "by constant and continuous labor lasting several weeks many important financial groups in this country were brought into association with this undertaking." Cromwell then incorporated in New Jersey, December 27, 1899, the Panama Canal Company of America.

The incorporators were William P. Chapman Jr., Henry W. Clark and Francis D. Pollak, all clerks, later partners or associates, in Cromwell's law office. Capital was to be $30,000,000, expandable to $120,000,000, covered by 5,000,000 first preferred, 15,000,000 second preferred and 10,000,000 common shares.

*The New York World,* the *New York Tribune* and the *New York Times* all published on December 28, 1899 long stories from details supplied by Cromwell's press bureau. Cromwell and Francis Lynde Stetson, known then to be one of J. P. Morgan's attorneys, were listed as counsel for the new company. The following were listed as among its financial backers

J. Edward Simmons, President of the Fourth National Bank, Kuhn, Loeb & Co.; E. C. Converse, President of the National Tube Company; Warner Van Norden, President of the Bank of North America, August Belmont, Levi P. Morton, J. & W. Seligman, Charles R. Flint, J. R. Delamar and Vernon H. Brown. Several of these names appear later as threads in the veils of mystery that through the years have shrouded the history of the Panama Canal and the Panama Republic.

Now while working up his "Americanization" program Cromwell was also busy getting the Republican Party to change its platform. In 1896 it was for building "The Nicaragua Canal." When he later billed his French clients for this political service he told them:

"We prevent the traditional endorsement of the Nicaragua route as a plank in the platform of the Republican Party, and we procure the substitution of the words AN ISTHMIAN CANAL .... This was an important step in our fight, since it freed the Republican Members of Congress from a party pledge and was the first occasion on which it was publicly recognized that a canal other than Nicaragua was possible."

What was done, and by whom, to "procure the substitution" of three words comes later in the untold story.

According to Cromwell, his on-paper Panama Canal Company of America never grew up because his "Americanization" project required final approval of the French company's stockholders and directors, and this was refused. Back of that refusal was the opposition of a French group headed by Baron Eugene Oppenheim. The Baron brought his own syndicating plan to New York. He got advice from the eminent attorney William M. Ivins, met Theodore Roosevelt's brother-in-law Douglas Robinson, and others; and returned to Paris to have the French Panama Canal management summarily dismiss Cromwell as general counsel. Cromwell's brief in 1907 gave only this explanation.

"July 1, 1901 — January 27, 1902. The Company, for reasons it deemed sufficient, ordered the cessation of all activities in the United States and itself took over the management, relieving us of all responsibility during that period."

It may be possible the French heard "rumors" that between May 25, 1900 and June 6, 1901 a "Memorandum of Agreement" was signed by sixteen American capitalists, banking houses and politicians to speculate in the securities of the bankrupt French Panama Canal Company, then purchasable directly or indirectly in the Paris market. How the document, alleged to be the duly-signed and witnessed original of that "Memorandum of Agreement," came into possession of Joseph Pulitzer's *World* is a later chapter in the untold story

Before his French clients suspended his services on June 30, 1901, Cromwell cabled them on June 25 that Admiral Walker had come to his office that day and would delay a final report of the Walker Commission if the French would submit an immediate and firm offer of outright sale instead of holding out for arbitration of price and terms. Cromwell had repeatedly urged this course.

The French again delayed, and the Walker Commission made its preliminary report, November 16, 1901, favoring Nicaragua. Cost of a canal at Panama would be prohibitive at the price suggested for arbitration Besides, there was the question whether Colombia would consent to a transfer of the French concession

Panicked by the Walker Commission's leaning toward Nicaragua, the French on January 4, 1902 cabled that they would accept the $40,000,000 price which the Walker Commission had suggested President Theodore Roosevelt, who had become a partisan of the Panama route, then reassembled the Walker Commission and asked it to reconsider Because of the definite offer from the French, the Walker Commission reported on January 18, 1902 that in view of changed conditions Panama would be the "most practicable and feasible" canal Commissioner Lewis M Haupt still believed Nicaragua would best serve United States interests How Theodore Roosevelt "persuaded" him to withdraw his dissent and sign with the majority is part of the untold story of Panama.

It was commonly reported at the time that Admiral Walker called Professor Haupt into the corridor outside the Commission's meeting and told him that President Theodore Roosevelt demanded a unanimous report because he feared that any dissent would be used to defeat all canal legislation.

Professor Haupt himself told me soon after I began my search for the real history of the Panama "revolution" that he was summoned to the White House and that President Roosevelt himself demanded a unanimous report Haupt signed — but insisted on putting into the minutes of the Walker Commission his reason, as follows·

"He still believed that the Nicaragua route was the better, but that the scope of the investigation had been expanded beyond the mere questions as to which route had the superior advantages, in view of the political situation and the great probability, if not certainty, of a divided report being used by the opponents of any canal to defeat legislation

"It was a question. therefore, of Panama or nothing. And as he believed firmly in the necessity of an Isthmian waterway for the general good, he had concluded that his duty to his country would be best fulfilled by waiving his objections and signing the report, with the understanding that this statement of his reasons be entered upon the minutes."

Three days after the Roosevelt prosecution of *The World* was quashed in the Federal court in New York, and before appeal for final adjudication had been taken to the United States Supreme Court, Professor Haupt in a hand-written note, which I still treasure, said to me "Coming so soon after our interview I was surprised that the Government had determined it was unwise to prosecute its suit and I hasten to contratulate you Yet the exposure might have been of great service to the *people* of this great nation, whose eyes should be opened to a few political policies. Your issue being quashed I presume your investigations will be pigeon-holed."

When the Roosevelt prosecution was finally killed by the Supreme Court in 1911 Professor Haupt wrote me again on April 1. 1911, in his clear script:

Dear Mr Harding

"He is thrice armed who has his quarrel just" provided the Court is not packed

Accept my congratulations and the hope that ere long the wheels of time may expedite the operations of the "law's delay" and give us a Government for the people and free from the interests — and the executive bureaus which control the patronage.

We need **Conservation** of mind as well as of matter. Our finanacial budgets might be **very** materially reduced **pro bono publico** and the appropriations expended with far greater efficiency for domestic commerce.

Very truly yours,<br>
LEWIS M HAUPT.

o o o

Nine days before the Walker Commission made its final report in favor of the Panama route the Hepburn Bill, committing the United States to Nicaragua, passed the House on January 9, 1902 by 309 to 2 Again it became apparent to some, though not all, of the French that only the astute and resourceful Cromwell could save them from complete disaster So a new management of the French company re-engaged Cromwell by cable, January 27, 1902.

According to Philippe Bunau-Varilla, French engineer and director-general of the Old Panama Canal Company on the Isthmus, this is how Cromwell was reinstated Bunau-Varilla said he interceded in Cromwell's behalf with the politically and financially powerful Senator Mark Hanna of Ohio and that Hanna was moved by J. Edward Simmons, who was banker for some of the Hanna business enterprises. Simmons was president of the Panama Railroad, Cromwell was its general counsel, and the railroad was still owned by the French canal company.

Cromwell's reinstatement as general counsel was confirmed by the new president of the French company, Marius Bo, in a letter of "instructions" dated January 27, 1902, **which read in part:**

"... But we require most expressly that no donations be made now or later, nor promises be made to anyone whomsoever which might bind the Company.... Result must be sought only by the most legitimate means, that in no case could we have recourse to methods as dangerous as they are unlawful, which consist principally in gifts or promises, of whatever nature they may be .. "

Why the injunction against "donations"? Liberal donations were never a strange toy for "Cromwell the Magnificent." Nor did liberal spending shock Bunau-Varilla, who worked intensively for the Panama cause while Cromwell was enjoying his seven months' suspension Bunau-Varilla was both sentimentally and financially interested. Duplicating at Panama what Ferdinand de Lesseps had achieved for the French at Suez was Bunau-Varilla's lifetime ambition He was also one of the "penalized stockholders" of the Old Panama Canal Company who had to subscribe for shares of the reorganization. With his brother Maurice he had a stake of 11,000 shares, par value 1,100,000 francs, in the New Panama Canal Company

Bunau-Varilla spent a fortune during 1900 and 1901 cultivating influential Americans and lectured before business and financial groups from coast to coast on the advantages of Panama over Nicaragua His efforts often paralleled those of Cromwell and his press bureau, particularly in spreading anti-Nicaragua propaganda by distributing Nicaragua postage stamps showing an active volcano near the route of the proposed canal Later Cromwell fed the same volcano scare material into Senate debates

Cromwell immediately after his reinstatement as general counsel, January 27, 1902, plunged into repairing the damages of seven months' hiatus in his lobbying and pressagenting His first move was to induce Senator Hanna to delay action in the Senate on the Hepburn Nicaragua Bill which had passed the House on January 9. Senator Hanna called before the Committee on Interoceanic Canals each member of the Walker Commission and plied him with questions which Cromwell said he supplied. "This," said Cromwell later, "monopolized our attention almost night and day for several weeks."

Cromwell also took credit for inspiring if not actually drafting the Spooner Bill as a substitute for the Hepburn Bill. Its enactment would require adoption of the Panama route provided a satisfactory treaty could be negotiated with Colombia. So Cromwell and several of his partners were continually in Washington supplying material for Senators' speeches in support of the "Hanna Minority Report" in favor of the Spooner Bill. The Hanna Report, said the Cromwell brief, became "the textbook on the Panama side" and "we had written the best part of it."

The Spooner Bill finally squeezed through the Senate, June 19, 1902, by 42 to 34 votes. "During every hour of this struggle," the Cromwell brief said in 1907, "at least two of the partners of our law firm, with other assistants, kept in constant consultation with Senators and assisted them. We passed in review every detail of the debates and every move in the matter which were the subject of advice and suggestions on our part. A slight difference of five votes would have killed the Panama Canal project and made the Nicaragua Canal the choice of the American people."

Then, after a struggle in conference, the House, which had been 309 to 2 for Nicaragua, gave in for the Spooner Bill because the attitude of the Senate conferees, coached by Cromwell and perhaps by Bunau-Varilla, was against any canal at all if not at Panama.

These were the circumstances under which — as President Theodore Roosevelt declared in his message of December 7, 1903 — the Panama route "commended itself to the deliberate judgment of the Congress"!

o o o

Now while Cromwell was juggling American legislation with one hand he was manipulating Colombian diplomacy with the other. According to his later claim for fees and disbursements, "one of the vital problems facing us" was to induce Colombia to bind itself by treaty to permit the New Panama Canal Company to transfer its about-to-lapse concession without paying over to Colombia as a transfer fee any portion of the $40,000,000 which Colombia would receive from the United States if a satisfactory treaty could be negotiated

So Cromwell "conceived the plan of inducing Colombia herself to intervene " The Colombian Government, he later said, "had no desire to assist in the sale" to the United States, so "Mr Cromwell personally and without cooperation opened negotiations with the Colombian Minister" and "in the course of conferences which succeeded each other for whole weeks at a time Mr. Cromwell led the Minister to pledge himself as to various bases of a proposal."

Then Cromwell himself drafted a treaty in which he was careful to provide that Colombia would permit the French canal company to transfer its Panama concession to the United States Then he re-drafted his first draft, "had it transmitted officially to the Secretary of State," and redrafted it again at Secretary Hay's request That was while Jose Vicente Concha, later President of Colombia, was its Minister in Washington. Concha refused to sign, and left his post in disgust

Concha's successor, Dr Tomas Herran, was instructed by his government to insist upon $10,000,000 lump sum and $600,000 annual rental "At last Mr Herran yielded to our arguments," said the later Cromwell brief, "and authorized us to offer to Mr Hay a compromise on the basis of $250,000." Cromwell hastily redrafted the proposed treaty, took it and Dr. Herran to Secretary Hay's house on the night of January 22, 1903, and there the Hay-Herran Treaty was signed. Cromwell, the sole witness, boasted that Secretary Hay gave him the pen and that he treasured it "as a precious souvenir of this incident."

The Cromwell brief in 1907 said "The entire negotiation of the treaty with Colombia was conducted by Mr. Cromwell with Ministers Concha and Herran and Secretary Hay, who held nearly all their official communications through his intermediary exclusively." Thus the historic Hay-Herran Treaty — whose later rejection by Colombia led to the birth of the Republic of Panama — was "initiated by Colombia" and was "entered into at the urgent solicitation of the people of Colombia." At least that was President Theodore Roosevelt's official version.

The day after the Hay-Herran Treaty was signed it was sent to the Senate on January 23, 1903. Many Senators demanded amendments to assure absolute control of the Canal Zone by the United States. Cromwell fought every change. He had been repeatedly advised by his agents in Bogota and had learned from Washington State Department cables — to which he claimed always to have access — that Colombia was preparing to exact from the French a fee of $10,000,000 for the privilege of transferring their non-transferable concession.

"It appeared to us," said Cromwell in his 1907 brief, "that the only way to escape these exactions, to defeat these maneuvers, and to save the company from paying a tribute of many millions of francs was to convince the American Government that it should refuse to consent to any amendment or to permit that the treaty should depend in any way on a previous agreement with the Canal Company, as Colombia was demanding. To this end we had numerous interviews with Secretary Hay, Senators Hanna, Spooner and Kittredge, Congressman Burton and others, and on certain occasions with the President We pointed out that Colombia had already pledged herself morally to consent, and that her consent should be imposed on her as being demanded by international good faith, and we thus created a feeling favorable to the support and protection of the company against these demands ...

"On several occasions the Secretary sent to the American Minister for transmission to the Colombian Government firm and positive refusals to consent to the amendment on transaction proposed Secretary Hay honored us with his confidence by permitting us to collaborate with him in writing these instructions."

Under these influences ratification of the Hay-Herran Treaty was jammed through the United States Senate March 17, 1903. Then came Cromwell's big problem: How to use the State Department to protect his French clients from having to give anything to Colombia for permission to transfer its property and concession to the United States.

The Colombian Congress was scheduled to meet on June 20, 1903 to consider the Hay-Herran Treaty Cromwell "suggested" to Secretary Hay on June 9 that the American Government should "announce to the Colombian Government in advance of the meeting of its Congress and with absolute frankness and firmness" that the United States relied upon "Colombia's treaty proposals and on the consent to the transfer included in these proposals."

The Cromwell brief in 1907 boasted that Secretary Hay accepted Cromwell's views and submitted them to President Theodore Roosevelt, that a few days later the President "sent for Mr Cromwell and after due consideration directed that instructions be sent to Colombia, which was done by Secretary Hay."

The Cromwell-inspired threat to Colombia, cabled from the State Department June 9, 1903, to A M. Beaupre, American Minister in Bogota, carried this ultimatum:

"The Colombian Government apparently does not appreciate the gravity of the situation. The canal negotiations were initiated by Colombia, and were energetically pressed upon this Government for several years The propositions presented by Colombia, with slight modifications, were finally accepted by us. In virtue of this agreement our Congress reversed its previous judgment and decided upon the Panama route.

"If Colombia should now reject the treaty or unduly delay its ratification, the friendly understanding between the two countries would be so seriously compromised that action might be taken by the Congress next winter which every friend of Colombia would regret Confidential. Communicate substance of this verbally to the Minister of Foreign Affairs. If he desires it, give him a copy in form of memorandum."

Cromwell was convinced, even when he inspired the ugly ultimatum of June 9, that Colombia would not ratify the Hay-Herran Treaty without amendments. On the very day the ultimatum was dispatched to Bogota, Cromwell had a long conference with President Theodore Roosevelt, as reported in the daily papers. Immediately after leaving the White House Cromwell sent his chief press agent, Roger L. Farnham, to *The World's* Washington bureau to inspire a long story — which *The World* innocently printed on the morning of June 14.

Farnham insisted, as he invariably did in many calls on *World* bureau writers, that his name should not be mentioned nor the source of the information be disclosed Charles S Albert, long a competent and trusted member of the Washington staff, detailed in the Farnham-inspired dispatch of June 14 the plans for creating a new nation on the Isthmus. Farnham told him that a delegation of five or six would soon come from Panama and give details to the State Department. Farnham continued frequently to inform Albert of Cromwellian developments in Bogota, Panama and Paris, always enjoining secrecy as to source. Many of the stories Albert wrote were for the information of *The World's* editors and were not published.

Even the exact date of the "revolution" was forecast by the Cromwell press agent in his conversation in the Washington bureau of *The World* on June 13, 1903. He said the blow would be struck — as it was — on November 3 because that was Election Day in the States and newspapers would be so crowded with election returns that an episode in Panama would command less attention.

Rejection of the Hay-Herran Treaty in Bogota hinged on nine amendments reported to the Colombian Senate. The main issues were: (1) over Colombia's insisting that the French should negotiate directly with Colombia for permission to transfer their concession, and (2) alienation of Colombia's sovereignty over the Canal Zone, which the Colombian Constitution forbade.

The Cromwell-inspired ultimatum of June 9 aroused a storm of indignation Conservative members of the Colombian Senate, from whom I later obtained intimate details, said no part of the national territory could be alienated without a Constitutional amendment, and that this could not be put through before the next session of their Congress So the Hay-Herran Treaty was rejected in Bogota on August 12, 1903 This news did not reach Washington by delayed cable until August 15.

The State Department was advised by cable from Minister Beaupre on August 31, 1903 that he had talked with a Senator who assured him that "if the United States will wait for the next session of Congress, the Canal can be secured without a revolution " But Cromwell and some others were not willing to wait

On hearing that nine treaty amendments had been reported to the Colombian Senate, President Theodore Roosevelt summoned Senator Shelby M Cullom, Chairman of the Senate Committee on Foreign Relations, to the Roosevelt summer-capital and home at Oyster Bay for conference on October 14 On leaving, Cullom gave an interview which the New York *Herald* printed. "We might make another treaty, not with Colombia but with Panama."

Propaganda spread the false story that the treaty amendments proposed in the Colombian Senate would require the United States to pay more than $40,000,000 for the property and rights of the New Panama Canal Company and $10,000,000 to Colombia The American Minister's cabled summary of the nine proposed amendments reached Washington on August 12 There was no suggestion that a transfer fee, demanded by Colombia, would be added to the price to be paid by the United States. Yet the State Department permitted the information to be broadcast through the press, uncontradicted, and with it built up sentiment against Colombia. Colombia was attempting to "hold up" Uncle Sam for more money! That misimpression persisted in the minds of millions of North Americans for a generation. Only to a very limited few, in midsummer 1903, went the order of the day On with the revolution!

*Chapter 3*

# Pre-Natal Labor in the Birth of a Republic

Cromwell had on the Isthmus both American and Panamanian employees and officers of the Panama Railroad dependent on his goodwill for their livelihood. They were accustomed to taking orders from him because he, as general counsel of the railroad and of its owner, the New Panama Canal Company of France, was virtually the head of the operation. These potential instruments for revolution were Jose Augustin Arango, land agent and local attorney for the railroad, who was also its lobbyist in Bogota as Senator representing the Department of Panama, Captain James R. Beers, freight agent and port captain, James R Shaler, superintendent, Herbert G. Prescott, assistant superintendent, and Dr. Manuel Amador Guerrero, the railroad's medical officer.

Senator Arango told some, but by no means all of the story of the "revolution" in his pamphlet, *"Data for a His-*

*tory of the Independence."* It was printed in pamphlet form in 1905. Telltale data in an earlier version were deleted. Even the 1905 pamphlet was removed from the Congressional Library in Washington. In it Arango said he refused to attend the 1903 session of the Colombian Congress because he was convinced the Hay-Herran Treaty would be rejected and that secession would be "the only way for the salvation of the Isthmus."

Arango's official version was that he sought out Captain Beers, "a man of entire trustworthiness and excellent judgment having influence with persons in high places," and asked him to go to New York. Also that "Captain Beers accepted the delicate mission and immediately left for the United States." The persons with influence in high places whom Beers knew were in Cromwell's office.

There was another version, known to several of Arango's co-conspirators and confirmed by them later to representatives of *The World.* It was that Senator Arango's first instructions were not to go to Bogota but to meet either Cromwell or his representative in Kingston, Jamaica, that this was changed to have Beers see Cromwell in New York. Nothing in Captain Beers' record indicated that he would leave his Panama Railroad job to seek revolutionary help without explicit approval from top authority.

Beers on returning to Panama August 4, 1903, "brought us very satisfactory news," the Arango pamphlet said. "He came well supplied with keys, codes and instructions from the friends who in that country were going to aid us when the movement started. Captain Beers subsequently also lent very important aid to the cause of our independence."

Others present at the secret meeting in Panama to receive his report said Beers told them he got his instructions and code from Cromwell, and that they could count on Cromwell's promise to "go the limit."

Then Dr. Amador, the Panama Railroad's medical officer, was put forward to give the revolutionary movement a native flavor. Ricardo Arias was to accompany Amador to

New York They were instructed to obtain from Cromwell and from official Washington direct confirmation of the promises of financial aid and military protection which Beers had reported The new commissioners were also told they must make sure of money in hand to finance the revolt.

The Arango pamphlet said Amador could go without exciting suspicion because of his family relationships. His son, Dr Raoul A Amador, was married in New York and was stationed at Fort Revere, Massachusetts, as an assistant surgeon with the United States Army. So Father Amador wrote Son Raoul to send a cable, "I am sick, come." The "sick" message arrived in time to equip Dr. Amador with a good alibi when he sailed from Colon August 26, 1903. (The history of Panama is sprinkled with planned alibis such as that one ) Ricardo Arias at the last moment found he could not go, so Dr Amador had to keep his own counsel until he arrived in New York September 1, 1903.

The Arango-Amador conspiracy by that time had been officially extended to include Ricardo Arias, a large land and cattle owner, Tomas Arias, who represented Charles R. Flint's American Trading & Development Company on the Isthmus, Carlos C Arosemena, Federico Boyd, a local capitalist, Manuel Espinosa B, Amador's brother-in-law, a retail druggist who was under contract to the Panama Railroad; and Nicanor A de Obarrio Unofficially, Captain Beers and Herbert G Prescott of the Panama Railroad were kept advised of every move and they in turn informed Cromwell or his agents.

The conspirators equipped Dr. Amador with codes for secret communication by cable, but no expense money. They expected North Americans would pay the cost of a revolution Being a good poker player, Amador won enough from fellow passengers to tide him over for several days but eventually had to borrow on his personal credit from the New York office of Joshua Lindo, a Panamanian merchant-banker.

Arriving in New York, Dr. Amador registered at the Hotel Endicott, Amsterdam Avenue at Eighty-first Street, and retained Room 152-C until his departure for Panama October 20 As an employee of the Panama Railroad, he first visited the company's New York office and, with its vice president, E. A. Drake, went to see Cromwell and present Arango's letter of introduction.

The Arango pamphlet omitted Cromwell's name, and described him only as "the respectable person who through Captain Beers had opened the way for our hopes." Cromwell biographers now say that he refused to see or assist Dr. Amador and that neither he nor his associates promoted the Panama "revolution." But Dr. Amador in his own carefully-edited account, written within a year of his death in 1909, said.

> The first interview was most cordial, and Mr. Cromwell made me a thousand offers in the direction of assisting us. But nothing could be done, he said, except when the Herran-Hay Treaty has been absolutely rejected, for in the end we believe it will be approved in spite of the great opposition of the houses of Congress. Vain were my efforts to convince Mr. Cromwell that no hope whatever should be entertained, and we continued the appointment to go on discussing the matter the following day

While Cromwell was telling Amador that he believed the treaty would be ratified in Bogota, he was telling J Gabriel Duque, owner of the Panama *Star & Herald* and of the Panama lottery, just the opposite. Duque came up on the same ship with Dr. Amador but they did not exchange confidences. Duque was taken to the Cromwell office by the press agent Farnham. Duque later told us that Cromwell said the treaty was dead and that Panama should make a revolution.

Duque went to Washington September 2, 1903. On advice of Farnham to avoid registering at a hotel, Duque went on the night train, waited for Secretary Hay to reach his office, conferred with him for two hours, and then paid a friendly visit to Colombian Minister Herran. Duque's son Carlos was married into a distinguished Colombian family and had prospered in his business in Bogota. Duque suggested to Dr. Herran that a word of caution to Bogota about the threat of a revolt in Panama might yet hasten approval of the Hay-Herran Treaty before it would expire by limitation on September 22.

Minister Herran immediately cabled his government that a revolt in Panama would probably have "powerful support" from the United States, and that "the Canal Company and Panama Railroad are deeply implicated." Dr. Herran put detectives on the trail of Dr Amador and wrote a note of warning to Cromwell and to the New Panama Canal Company that Colombia would hold them responsible for any secessionist plot in Panama.

The Arango historical pamphlet said the Herran warning "influenced so unfavorably the soul of the responsible gentleman with whom our representative had come to an understanding, that he evaded from that time, on various occasions, a meeting with Dr Amador, and there was produced a notable change in his conduct."

Dr Amador's earlier and unedited account, given orally to his fellow conspirators when he reported to them on his return from New York, said Cromwell discussed every phase of the situation in his first and second conferences, but refused to see Amador on two subsequent visits. When Amador waited and intercepted Cromwell in his outer office, Cromwell excitedly told him he would have nothing to do with the independence and pushed Amador out the door.

Then, for the record, to protect his French clients, Cromwell on September 10, 1903 cabled Colonel James R. Shaler, Superintendent of the Panama Railroad, to "take extra and every precaution to strictly perform our obligations to Colombia under concession and instruct officials and employees to be careful as heretofore not to participate in any movements or hostilities whatever .... in order to prevent even a pretext for complaint or claim by the Bogota or Panama governments . . (signed) Cromwell, General Counsel."

Having covered himself by that alibi, Cromwell sailed for Paris, October 15, "to confer rapidly and return." He arrived in Paris October 23 and did not return to New York until November 17. Meanwhile Bunau-Varilla took over where Cromwell ostensibly left off.

Bunau-Varilla's official version, as told in his encyclopedic book of Panama adventures published in London in 1913, boils down to this His arrival in New York September 22, 1903 was by "a chance incident that was to have incalculable consequences." Bunau-Varilla had caused a prophetic and warning article to be published, September 2, 1903 in the Paris newspaper *Le Matin* He said he sent a copy "under sealed envelope" to President Theodore Roosevelt at Oyster Bay, and that he intended "to await in Paris the revival of political activity in Washington." He arrived in New York several weeks ahead of his schedule solely because his wife was afraid to cross the Atlantic alone, and she was sailing to join their 13-year-old son, a victim of hay fever, who was summering on the Maine coast with the daughter of Bunau-Varilla's old friend John Bigelow, retired American Minister to France

So it would appear that the astute and resourceful Cromwell, having invested ten years and hundreds of thousands of dollars in time in the Panama enterprise, fled to Paris without knowing for a certainty what competent hand would be there to guide and finance the "revolution"

Back in 1902 Cromwell telegraphed a cordial note of thanks and cooperation to Bunau-Varilla for having interceded with Senator Hanna to get Cromwell reinstated as general counsel of the French company But at the end both denied they were cooperating when Cromwell left for Paris and Bunau-Varilla stepped in to carry through the revolutionary plan.

The Cromwell brief said, four years later, that the gap

was filled by one of Cromwell's partners, William J. Curtis and that Curtis "took up the management of the company's interests, of which we notified the President and Secretary of State by letter." Also that from Paris on October 31, 1903 Cromwell cabled President Theodore Roosevelt that the French company's management "express to you their entire confidence in the success of your masterful policy. I have received full powers to complete all details on my coming return."

Bunau-Varilla on arriving in New York September 22 registered at the Waldorf-Astoria, went immediately to see Joshua Lindo, the Panamanian merchant-banker, and was told that Cromwell had renegged on all his promises to Amador. Crushed by Cromwell's rebuff — so Bunau-Varilla recorded in 1913 — Amador went to see him at the Waldorf-Astoria the very next day. Bunau-Varilla's story was that he assured Amador, then went to Washington, saw Secretary of State John Hay and Assistant Secretary Francis B. Loomis, and was taken by Loomis to the White House for a conference with President Roosevelt on October 9.

Bunau-Varilla said he told the President that a revolution in Panama was certain. Then, by his own deductions, he figured out that the United States would not permit Colombia to put down a revolt, and that Amador should sail for Panama on October 20 to carry out the safe "revolution" under the guns of the United States Navy. Bunau-Varilla in his 1913 volume set forth in quotation marks what Amador said and what Bunau-Varilla said in such detail as to suggest that a then-non-existent tape-recorder was at hand. Taking to himself full credit for putting over the "revolution" and creating the Republic of Panama, Bunau-Varilla quoted himself as saying to Amador:

"The moment has come to clear the deck for action . . . I can give you the assurance that you will be protected by the American forces forty-eight hours after you have proclaimed the new Republic of the Isthmus . . ." I take the responsibility of it. I take also the responsibility of obtaining for you, from a bank, or of furnishing you myself, the one hundred thousand dollars which are necessary to you . . . . I have prepared the programme of military operations, the Declaration of Independence, a base for the Constitution of the new Republic, and finally a code with which to correspond with me . It will be necessary to entrust me with the diplomatic representation of the new Republic at Washington."

Mme. Bunau-Varilla patched together the makeshift Panama flag, which Dr Amador wrapped around his waist and delivered to his fellow conspirators the evening after he arrived in Colon on October 27. Herbert G. Prescott, assistant superintendent of the Panama Railroad, alone met Amador at the pier. He told Prescott that Bunau-Varilla had promised to have American warships on hand to protect Panama from Colombia The documents that Bunau-Varilla had given to Dr. Amador were entrusted to Captain Beers' son, George K Beers, purser of the S. S. Yucatan on which Amador came from New York.

In anticipation of trouble on the Isthmus United States Army officers, disguised as civilians, were in Panama and Colon and in the interior mapping possible offensive and defensive positions. President Theodore Roosevelt in October ordered the General Staff to report on what forces would be needed to hold the coastal towns On October 16 he personally interviewed Captain C. B. Humphrey and Lieutenant Grayson Mallet-Prevost Murphy Then three more "observers" were dispatched to Panama Captain Sidney A. Cloman passed as "S. A. Otts, lumberman;" Captain William G Hahn as "H E. Howard, mining engineer," and Major Guy L. Edie, medical officer, as "G. E. Edie, New York capitalist." Hahn, alias Howard, with letters of introduction to Dr Amador, made himself socially acceptable by playing poker with Captain Beers, whom he knew as Cromwell's confidential man.

Even before Dr. Amador could report to his revolutionary junta at Federico Boyd's house on the evening of October 27 the U.S.S. Dixie had been ordered to load 450 marines and be ready to sail from League Island "about the 23rd." And by October 24 U.S.S. Nashville had been ordered to load coal and proceed to Kingston. U.S. Navy ships were also heading south from San Francisco, under sealed orders.

All-important to the men of the revolutionary junta, next to being saved from the wrath of the Colombian Government, was how to meet the expenses On October 26 — three days after Cromwell arrived in Paris — the Credit Lyonnais by cable to Heidelbach, Ickelheimer & Co of New York opened in favor of Bunau-Varilla a credit of $100,000. Bunau-Varilla always contended that this near-proximity of dates did not mean that he and Cromwell were cooperating.

Just how the Panama "revolution" was financed may always remain part of the untold story Many versions have persisted for half a century But dissatisfaction with Dr. Amador's report to the revolutionary junta at Federico Boyd's house on the evening of October 27, 1903, was indelibly remembered and told and re-told.

Dr Amador outlined the plan agreed upon between him and Bunau-Varilla. Only the Canal Zone and the terminal cities of Panama and Colon would be declared independent The United States Government would recognize this new nation as the "Republic of the Isthmus." Amador's unfurling of the proposed Panama flag, sewed together in New York by Mme. Bunau-Varilla, brought a storm of protest. It was an American flag with the jack cut out and in its place on a blue silk ground two stars were joined by a narrow strip of white ribbon indicative of the Canal.

Ricardo Arias interrupted the flag criticism to denounce the exclusion of the rest of the Department of Panama. In common with other substantial landowners, he would be ruined if his property was not protected from Colombian reprisal. Amador said he had reported only what had been suggested in Washington, and he was sure the United States would not let Colombian troops attack any part of

Panama. Tomas Arias and Federico Boyd joined the dissenters. Prescott, the only American in the meeting, was silent. The meeting broke up around 11 o'clock and Dr. Amador went home to share his concern with his cool-headed wife, Maria de la Ossa de Amador

On the following day Tomas Arias went to Amador and told him he did not wish to go along with the plan as he was afraid it would not turn out well and he would suffer more than anyone else Amador tried to reassure him, but Arias replied in phrases almost identical with statements made by other revolutionaries in 1909 Arias told Amador that both he and Jose Agustin Arango were "old men and don't care — but I do care, I don't like to be hung."

Seeing that Tomas Arias was determined to withdraw and that his disaffection would undoubtedly start a panic among the others, Amador offered to send a cable to obtain more certain assurance that American warships would be on hand. He asked Arias to await a reply Then he went to Prescott, told him of the Arias threat, and on Prescott's advice sent the following cable to Bunau-Varilla in their private code.

"FATE NEWS BAD POWERFUL TIGER URGE VAPOR COLON."

Transalted, this message read

"WE HAVE NEWS OF ARRIVAL OF COLOMBIAN FORCES BY ATLANTIC IN FIVE DAYS MORE THAN TWO HUNDRED. URGE WARSHIP FOR COLON."

Bunau-Varilla hurried to Washington, saw Assistant Secretary of State Loomis and, stopping off in Baltimore at noon of October 30, sent from there his cabled answer to Amador.

"THIRTY-SIX HOURS ATLANTIC, FORTY-EIGHT PACIFIC."

And the American warships arrived as scheduled.

The Nashville, as per Bunau-Varilla's promise, arrived at Colon November 2 at 5 30 P.M. The same day, by direction of President Theodore Roosevelt, Acting Secretary of the Navy Charles Hal Darling cabled the commanders of the Nashville at Colon and the Dixie, not yet arrived from Kingston, to "maintain free and uninterrupted transit If interruption threatened by armed forces, occupy the line of railroad Prevent landing of any armed forces .." And the Dixie's commander was cabled to "proceed with all possible dispatch from Kingston to Colon Government force reported approaching the Isthmus in vessels. Prevent their landing if in your judgment this would precipitate conflict." And the commanders of the Marblehead at Acapulco, Mexico, and the Boston at San Juan del Sur, Nicaragua, were ordered to 'proceed with all possible dispatch to Panama If doubtful as to the intention of any armed forces, occupy Ancon Hill strongly with artillery."

But before these orders could be delivered to the Navy commanders, 500 Colombian troops under Generals Juan B Tovar and Ramon G Amaya arrived at Colon aboard the Colombian gunboat Cartegena at 11.30 P M of November 2

News of the unexpected arrival of so many Colombian troops was telephoned from Colon to Prescott, who was in Panama keeping in constant touch with Amador. The conspirators almost lost heart, but the resolute wife of Dr. Amador told them it was too late to draw back It was hastily agreed that Colonel Shaler should bring over the Colombian generals and isolate their soldiers in Colon Prescott had provided for this emergency by shifting all rollingstock to the Panama end of the line If troops did get a train by force, Prescott had planned to have their arms stacked in the rear car, then have it cut off on the way over and deliver unarmed soldiers into the hands of the rebels in Panama. If worse came to worst, Prescott would have a dynamite gang blow up the train at Miraflores. His brother Richard, also a Panama Railroad employee, would be on hand — as he was — to cut telephone and telegraph communications

So "Independence Day" dawned with Colonel Shaler at

the Colon dock to welcome Generals Tovar and Amaya and escort them to seats in a special car. To their protest he replied that the troops would be on the next train. Then he blew a whistle himself and started the train to Panama, while he remained in Colon.

Meanwhile General Esteban Huertas, commander of the Colombian garrison in Panama, had been taken into the conspiracy — with ample promises His small command had been depleted by sending Colonel Leoncio Tascon, who was believed to be loyal to Bogota, and 100 of his men to the interior town of Penonome to suppress a "reported" but non-existent invasion from Nicaragua.

Huertas with military escort welcomed Tovar and Amaya at the railroad station in Panama. The Governor's coach took them downtown and they were entertained from noon until 5:30 P. M., when Huertas gave the order. Tovar and Amaya were surrounded with fixed bayonets and told they were prisoners of the revolution. At 6 P. M. Arango, Tomas Arias and Federico Boyd assumed charge as a "Junta of Government" and immediately notified Colonel Shaler, as superintendent of the Panama Railroad, that the new entity, to be known as "The Republic of the Isthmus," would assume all obligations under the contract between the railroad company and Colombia At the same time Commander Hubbard of the Nashville ordered Shaler not to transport either Colombian or revolutionary troops

The only unplanned incident was the firing of five or six shells from the Colombian gunboat Bogota in Panama harbor. Its commander threatened to bombard the city if the Colombian generals were not released, but soon changed his mind. During the bombardment the Panama City Council was meeting and resolving to support the Provisional Government.

Prompt decisions were needed, for Colonel Eliseo Torres, in command of the troops stranded in Colon, was threatening to burn the town. No clashes resulted. Torres agreed to take his 500 soldiers back to Colombia provided he got

$8,000 for himself and a guarantee that passage for his men on the Royal Mail steamer Orinoco would be forthcoming. Prescott appealed to the Junta, but it had used up all the credit it could then command from local bankers to pay off Huertas and his men. So Prescott approved using $8,000 from the safe of the Panama Railroad in Colon, and the passage money was guaranteed by the signatures of Shaler for the railroad, Porfirio Melendez for the Provisional Government, and Commander Hubbard for the United States Navy.

News of the "spontaneous uprising" at Panama was withheld from North American newspapers until late at night November 3 As forecast by Cromwell's press agent Farnham back in midsummer, the "revolution" escaped conspicuous publicity in competition with election news. The *New York Herald* gave almost its entire front page to the election of George B. McClellan as Mayor of New York, under eight-column headlines Buried in a lower corner was a short dispatch from its Isthmian correspondent, Samuel Boyd, brother of Federico. It was labeled "New York Herald Cable, Panama, Colombia, via Galveston, Texas." The heading was: "Panama Taken by Rebels, Independence Declared Successful Revolution Coup Effected, War Ships at the Port Are Seized and Colombian Officials Are Prisoners."

Early on November 4 Dr. Amador made a rabble-rousing speech to General Huertas and his soldiers. Bribe money, obtained from local bankers, was paid promptly, and soon the soldiers and a mob of civilians were carrying Huertas in a chair around the plaza flanked by Dr. Amador carrying the new Panama flag and by Felix Ehrman, acting United States Consul General, carrying the Stars and Stripes. The parade ended with bottles of champagne doused on the head of the General of the Revolution The price of this new loyalty was $50 (silver, worth 50 cents in American money) per soldier, and, later, in thousands of silver dollars, according to rank of the Huertas lieutenants, up to $30,000 silver for Huertas. Later the Amador Government retired

Huertas on a grant of $50,000 gold.

With a similar setting early in the afternoon of November 4 the patriots assembled in solemn session in the Municipal Council. They recognized Arango, Arias and Boyd as their Provisional Government, rejected the designation "Republic of the Isthmus" and elected as the Cabinet of the about-to-be Republic of Panama: Secretary of Government, Eusebio A. Morales; Secretary of War and Navy, Nicanor A. de Obarrio; Secretary of Foreign Affairs, Francisco V. de la Espriella; Secretary of Treasury, Manuel E. Amador; Secretary of Justice, Carlos A. Mendoza; Secretary of Public Instruction, Julio J. Fabrega. They also listed General H. O. Jeffries, Commander of the gunboat Twenty-first of November, as one of the officials of the Provisional Government. When the Hay-Bunau-Varilla Treaty was formally ratified, December 4, 1903, Francisco Antonio Facio, as sub-secretary, signed in place of Fabrega.

The patriots then adjourned to a massmeeting in Cathedral Plaza to hear the Panama Declaration of Independence read from the Cathedral steps by their newly-elected Secretary of Justice, Carlos A. Mendoza.

Bunau-Varilla received his first direct news by cable from Dr. Amador at 10 P.M. of November 3. By 11:45 he was on the night train for Washington. He conferred with Assistant Secretary of State Loomis, but still lacking his promised diplomatic powers, he returned to New York and continued for two days to demand them by cable. His urgent messages were crossed by equally urgent demands from Amador for the $100,000 which he said Bunau-Varilla had promised. Finally Bunau-Varilla came through with $25,000 and the Provisional Government of Panama cabled Washington on November 6 that Bunau-Varilla had been appointed "Envoy Extraordinary with full powers to conduct diplomatic and financial negotiations."

On the same day, November 6, Colonel Torres, having received his reward of $8,000 from the safe of the Panama Railroad in Colon and guaranteed passage for his troops'

### Pre-Natal Labor in the Birth of a Republic

return to Colombia, brought the War of Independence to its apparent end Formal celebration in Colon was scheduled for the morning of November 7. A resolution of adhesion to the Provisional Government passed by the Colon Municipal Council was read, also the Manifesto of the Junta and the Declaration of Independence. Then the new flag of the Republic of Panama was hoisted by Major William Murray Black, U S A, and the crowd cheered "Viva la Republica! Vivan los Americanos!

So was born the little Republic whose radicals now cry: "Gringos, go home!"

*Chapter 4*

# The Baby Republic Is Born

At 12.51 P. M. of November 7, 1903 Secretary of State Hay cabled instructions to United States Vice Consul General Felix Ehrman in Panama to enter into relations with the de facto government. At 1.40 P. M. Secretary Hay received Bunau-Varilla's telegram from New York announcing that "the Republic of Panama has been pleased to designate me as its Envoy Extraordinary and Minister Plenipotentiary near the Government of the United States" and that "in spreading her protecting wings over the territory of our Republic the American Eagle has sanctified it."

Bunau-Varilla's authority was already in jeopardy. Dr. Amador cabled him — so wrote Bunau-Varilla in his 1913 book of Panama adventures — that his powers would be limited to those of a "Confidential Agent," and Arango, Boyd and Arias instructed him by cable to contract a loan of $200,000. Bunau-Varilla said he ignored these instructions as beneath his dignity.

A newspaper story that a special commission would soon

leave Panama and do the treaty negotiating gave Bunau-Varilla the weapon he needed to belabor Secretary Hay to rush a treaty to conclusion. On November 13, 1903 President Theodore Roosevelt received Bunau-Varilla at the White House and extended formal recognition to the new Republic of Panama. By November 15 Secretary Hay sent to Bunau-Varilla a copy of the Hay-Herran Treaty, which Colombia had rejected, modified to apply to Panama.

Bunau-Varilla, according to his later story, worked all night redrafting and strengthening Secretary Hay's draft. His handling of the question of sovereignty is still a burning issue in Panama, and should be carefully noted here. Bunau-Varilla wrote in his 1913 book:

"After mature thought I recognized that if I enumerated in succession the various attributes of sovereignty granted, I ran the risk of seeing, in the Senate, some other attributes asked for To cut short any possible debate I decided to grant a concession of sovereignty en bloc." The formula which Bunau-Varilla said seemed to him the best was expressed in his text of Article III of the Hay-Bunau-Varilla Treaty. The sovereignty of the United States within the Panama Canal Zone, despite Panamanian clamor for its abrogation, still stands.

*Article III, Hay-Bunau-Varilla Treaty of 1903*

"The Republic of Panama grants to the United States all the rights, power and authority within the zone mentioned and described in Article II of this agreement and within the limits of all auxiliary lands and waters mentioned and described in said Article II which the United States would possess and exercise if it were the sovereign of the territory within which said lands and waters are located to the entire exclusion of the exercise by the Republic of Panama of any such sovereign rights, power or authority "

In contrast, the rejected Hay-Herran Treaty provided: "The rights and privileges granted to the United States by the terms of this convention shall not affect the sovereignty of the Republic of Colombia over the territory within whose boundaries such rights and privileges are to be exercised. The United States freely acknowledges and recognizes this sovereignty and disavows any intention to impair it in any way whatever . . . "

Bunau-Varilla recorded in his 1913 book that at 10 P. M. of November 17, 1903 he sent a note to Secretary Hay at his residence and on Mr. Hay's immediate response had a long conference that night preliminary to the final re-typing of the treaty in the State Department on the 18th. Bunau-Varilla wrote in 1913 that he condensed his impressions as to the necessity for acting rapidly in these words to Secretary Hay. "So long as the delegation [Amador and Boyd] has not arrived in Washington I shall be free to deal with you alone, provided with complete and absolute powers. When they arrive I shall no longer be alone. In fact I may perhaps soon no longer be here at all."

Bunau-Varilla later confided to history that, with the assistance of Frank D. Pavey, an American lawyer whom he appointed counsel to the Panama Legation in Washington, he wrote the entire treaty Also that Amador and Boyd came from Panama "under pretense of furnishing me with advice, but in reality to make the treaty themselves." Further Bunau-Varilla accounted for Amador's dissatisfaction as being due to personal ambition He said Amador objected when Bunau-Varilla told him before leaving for Panama in October to make the "revolution" that Bunau-Varilla insisted on being himself the first Minister, for Amador wanted that honor for himself.

Whatever may have been the secret motives of their journey, Amador and Boyd arrived from Colon on the steamer City of Washington early in the morning of November 17, 1903 Cromwell's Man Friday, Farnham, went down the bay on a revenue cutter and escorted them to the old Fifth Avenue Hotel. There they were registered from the morning of the 17th to 3 30 P. M of the 18th. Amador spent the night at the home of his son, Dr. Raoul A. Amador, 216 West 112th Street.

## The Baby Republic Is Born

Cromwell four years later in his brief to the French arbitrators of his fee said "Before leaving Panama these personages had arranged by cable to meet Mr Cromwell in New York for a conference, Mr Cromwell being on his way at the same time from Paris to New York. An important conference which lasted a whole day followed, in the course of which we obtained the assurance that the concessions and property of the Panama Canal Co on the Isthmus would be fully recognized and protected."

New York papers reported that Cromwell was closeted with Amador and Boyd at their hotel for an hour, and quoted Cromwell and Boyd as saying the call was purely social, that Cromwell came simply to congratulate the patriots. Boyd's denial under oath in 1909 that he and Amador saw Cromwell on their arrival in New York is a later incident.

Knowing that Amador and Boyd were in New York, Bunau-Varilla sent them a "telegram of welcome, apologizing for not being able to go and meet them." Then he hastened to obtain an appointment to be at Secretary Hay's home to sign, at 6:40 P. M. of November 18, 1903, the historic Hay-Bunau-Varilla Treaty. Next, at 7.15 P. M. Bunau-Varilla cabled his government in Panama that the treaty had been signed, and that the special commissioners would arrive in Washington "in about two hours." He welcomed them at the Washington station and broke the news: they had arrived too late!

According to Bunau-Varilla, Dr. Amador was so incensed and disappointed that "he nearly swooned on the platform of the station," and Boyd "pretended that fresh negotiations on certain points would have to be opened with the Department of State."

How far the cleavage had spread was disclosed in Bunau-Varilla's book. He quoted a peremptory cable received by him from his government at 10.55 P. M. of November 19. ".. inform us of the cause which led you to sign the treaty before conferring with the delegates Amador and Boyd. Communicate to us the modifications introduced."

Convinced that Amador and Boyd were conspiring to have Panama delay, amend or even reject his treaty, Bunau-Varilla on November 25 cabled a long ultimatum, saying in effect, "You ratify or I resign." Opposition in Panama then faded or went underground. The treaty was ratified by Decree No. 24 at 11:30 A. M. December 2, 1903 and was signed by each member of the Cabinet of the Provisional Government. It was submitted to the United States Senate on December 7, 1903, but long and bitter debate continued until February 23, 1904, when ratification without amendment was voted, 65 to 15. Ratifications were exchanged between Secretary Hay and Minister Bunau-Varilla at 11 A M. February 25, 1904, and thereupon Bunau-Varilla cabled his resignation to Panama.

During these exciting days when the swadling clothes of the baby Republic were being adjusted, Cromwell was busier than ever His trusted lieutenant, Herbert G. Prescott, the assistant superintendent of the Panama Railroad whom Amador thanked as his "first aid de camp," was commissioned by the Junta immediately after the "revolution" to transmit to President Theodore Roosevelt the precious first flag of the Republic. Prescott knew it should go through Cromwell's hands.

So, while busy coaching Amador and Boyd and having them meet the right men in Washington in preparation for the forthcoming debate in the Senate on ratification or rejection of the Hay-Bunau-Varilla Treaty, Cromwell took time to dispatch from New York on November 30, 1903 this cable:

H. G. Prescott, Panama

Inform Municipal Council and Junta I had honor and pleasure presenting to President Roosevelt the flag of the Republic, forwarded through you. Among other things, I remarked that while the United States would never part with its historic Liberty Bell, which first rang out the independence of this nation and the reverberation of which continues to be an inspiration to all liberty-loving people, yet so fond was the gratitude and affection of the Republic of Panama to the President that they gave into his hands their most precious treasure, the sacred and historic flag, the first raised upon the Declaration of Independence. The President accepted the gift in most enthusiastic and grateful terms, and requested me to convey his unbounded thanks and pleasure, and to say he designs having a suitable inscription woven upon its surface to perpetuate its historic character and the grateful acts of its donors. I greet you all.

WILLIAM NELSON CROMWELL

As told later by Cromwell in his brief, after his "all-day conference" with Amador and Boyd in New York on November 18, 1903, "at their request we met these personages in Washington to assist in taking up pending questions."

In order to assure ratification of the Hay-Bunau-Varilla Treaty, Cromwell said, "we arranged interviews between the special delegates [Amador and Boyd] and Senators Hanna, Fairbanks, Kittredge, Platt and other Members of Congress . . During their stay in Washington and New York, which lasted a long time, the special delegates conferred daily with one or several of our partners, asked and followed our advice on all phases of the unique situation . . We were relied upon to devote ourselves to the ratification of the treaty and we devoted ourselves to this task during the six following weeks with every resource at our command . We prepared an exhaustive statement of the unjust wrongs that Panama had suffered for a period of 50 years, which statement we communicated to the government officials and Members of Congress to justify the independence...."

Cromwell's "exhaustive statement of unjust wrongs" inflicted upon Panama was later attacked by Colombian historians and riddled for its inaccuracies. Even more severely Cromwell and his inaccuracies were denounced later by Bunau-Varilla. The French engineer-diplomat's interest back in 1902 in interceding with Senator Mark Hanna to get Cromwell reinstated as general counsel for the French canal promoters was tempered, at first, by growing distrust, then by bitter hatred when he learned that Cromwell's press agent, Jonas Whitley, brought to *The World* background material for stories about Bunau-Varilla's alleged part in American speculation in the securities of the bankrupt French company

Bunau-Varilla also charged in his 1913 book that Cromwell used Vice President E. A. Drake of the Panama Railroad at the New York end and Captain James R. Beers at the Panama end as coverups of his campaign to discredit Bunau-Varilla and have him removed as Panama's Minister. A cable message from Drake to Beers dated New York, November 30, 1903 said Bunau-Varilla was "trying to disturb the Junta" by reports 'that there is great danger that Washington will make a trade with Reyes and withdraw warships ..."

This was a reference to the mission of General Rafael Reyes and other Colombian leaders to negotiate peace, and to the patrolling of Panama's Atlantic and Pacific coasts by United States Navy craft to prevent any attempt by Colombia to retake the Isthmus. These military activities went so far as to land United States forces at Yavisa, in the eastern end of Panama, but this was soon countermanded.

The Drake cable to Beers went on

"Mr Cromwell has direct assurance from President Roosevelt, Senator Hanna and other Senators that there is not the slightest danger of this. Evidently the Minister's [Bunau-Varilla's] pretense of influence is grossly exaggerated. We have fullest support of Mr. Cromwell and his friends who have carried every victory for past six years. Junta evidently do not know that objection exists in Washington to the Minister    Cable me.   when will Junta appoint Pablo Arosemena [as Minister, replacing Bunau-Varilla]Answer today if possible. DRAKE."

While supplying Republican Senators with arguments to meet attacks on the pending treaty by Senator Morgan and

## The Baby Republic Is Born

other critics, Cromwell was also cultivating General Reyes. He later told the arbitrators of his claim for fees that Reyes met him in New York "for a series of conferences which later were of great importance and in the course of which a warm friendship sprang up, a friendship which still endures." (September 5, 1907)

Cromwell said in his brief that "we do not consider ourselves at liberty to set forth here the details of these conferences, but we can mention that General Reyes gave them such great consideration and encouragement that we at once sent Captain Beers to the Isthmus to explain the plan in detail to the Government of Panama, which promptly authorized its study." The result, for which Cromwell took full credit, was the signing of the protocol of a tri-partite treaty of peace between Colombia, Panama and the United States, August 17, 1907. This treaty was repudiated by Colombia and Reyes, who had risen to the Presidency, was discredited and driven into exile.

Throughout the period of the long and bitter debate in the Senate over ratification of the Hay-Bunau-Varilla Treaty, Navy and Marine forces of the United States were on both coasts of Panama actively preparing to defend the independence. Cooperation went so far as to provide Navy vessels small enough to penetrate little inlets. One of these escorted representatives of the Junta to the little town of David, near the Costa Rican border, to persuade that pro-Colombian community to accept the unwanted independence.

On the surface, hostilities practically disappeared after ratification of the Hay-Bunau-Varilla Treaty by the United States Senate on February 23 and its formal proclamation on February 26, 1904. But as late as 1909 chiefs of the San Blas Indians at the eastern end of the Isthmus were still avowing their loyalty to Colombia.

The United States still had to get title to the property of the New Panama Canal Company on the Isthmus and in return deliver $40,000,000 to the owners of the bonds of the Old Panama Canal Company and the shares of the New Panama Canal Company — whoever they might be, also to deliver $10,000,000 to the Republic of Panama instead of the $10,000,000 which would have gone to Colombia.

How all this was accomplished, and who really go the money, continued to be intermittent subjects of rumor and recrimination and political controversy — until Cromwell's self-defensive charge of attempted blackmail on October 1, 1908 led President Theodore Roosevelt to launch his misfired missile at Joseph Pulitzer of *The World* and the publishers of the *Indianapolis News*. Then began the slow unfolding of the untold story of Panama.

*Chapter 5*

# *Theodore Roosevelt Challenges a Free Press*

After Senator Morgan's earlier failure to probe to the bottom of the Panama mess and in 1904 to block ratification of the Hay-Bunau-Varilla Treaty, public interest became engrossed in the bigness of the Panama Canal and its military and commercial importance. Well-publicized accounts of how "T. R. is making the dirt fly" helped to create an atmosphere jealous of further investigation and impatient of criticism.

Many editors came to feel that the Panama Canal had become sacrosanct and that the public could not differentiate between exposure and condemnation of the lawless acquisition of the Canal Zone and attacks on the Canal enterprise itself. As I said to the Latin-American Conference at Clark University, November 18, 1913, "there was a long period during which intelligent discussion and honest criticism of the Panama affair was so unpopular as to be almost entirely suppressed."

That was the situation when, at the height of the 1908 campaign to elect William Howard Taft as President Theodore Roosevelt's successor, the astute Cromwell made his momentous miscalculation. Cromwell feared publicity as much as he valued its power. He had spent countless thousands of dollars to create it, as well as to suppress it. He had assembled a vast publicity and lobbying organization for his French canal clients and had billed them for its cost. The Paris arbitrators' cutting of his bill from $832,449.38 to $228,282.71 was still fresh in his memory.

Now, fearing a renewal of political attacks in the presidential campaign in which he was active, and having valuable financial ties with the new Panama Republic, Cromwell sent to bat, not his publicity experts but his ranking law partner, William J. Curtis. By this time Cromwell had become senior partner and dominating personality of the partnership founded in 1879 by Algernon Sydney Sullivan and Cromwell, who was then only 25 years old.

Curtis went to see William Travers Jerome, District Attorney of New York on October 1, 1908 to lodge Cromwell's complaint that certain persons were trying to blackmail him about Panama. The Democratic National Committee had made the Panama scandal a campaign issue by its published statement of August 29, 1908. It pointed to Cromwell, "probably the most conspicuous trust lawyer in this country," as a close associate of Taft, the presidential nominee, and a member of the G.O.P.'s national executive committee. It described Cromwell as "attorney for the Panama Canal combine, Kuhn, Loeb & Co., the Harriman interests, the sugar trust, Standard Oil trust, et al."

News of the Curtis call on Jerome leaked into *The World* on October 2, 1908 and Allen Sangree, an experienced reporter, was sent to get the facts. Sangree saw Jerome, who said Curtis had called on him "regarding certain matters which he was not at liberty to give out." Sangree then went to Cromwell's office. Sangree's written memorandum, which is still in my files, said Cromwell was courteous but "had nothing to say." Sangree returned to the newsroom emptyhanded.

Normally, the blackmail story would have died then. But Cromwell, to make doubly sure, sent his second-string publicity man, Jonas Whitley, who, as a former employee knew World editors, to see Caleb M Van Hamm, Mr Pulitzer's managing editor He told Van Hamm that the story he was about to publish would be libelous and dangerous

Verifying first that no facts were in hand and that no Panama story was in preparation, Van Hamm listened as Whitley voluntarily related the substance of the Cromwell-Curtis complaint It was that Cromwell and Bunau-Varilla had formed a speculative syndicate to buy up the French canal securities and unload them, at tremendous profit, when the Panama Canal became property of the United States

The political dynamite in the story, said Whitley, was the allegation that participants in the syndicate were Charles P. Taft, brother of William Howard Taft, the G. O. P. candidate for the Presidency, and Douglas Robinson, brother-in-law of President Theodore Roosevelt Whitley, without naming them, said that certain individuals were threatening to exploit the details unless Cromwell bought them off.

Van Hamm then went to his inside office, dictated to his stenographer details as Whitley had related them, and after the story was typed brought it out to Whitley for possible correction Whitley crossed out Charles P Taft's name, substituted that of Henry W Taft, then changed it back to Charles P Taft Whitley then read the text over a newsroom telephone to Cromwell, who approved it, and in that form the story was printed the following morning, October 3, 1908

Late that night Cromwell telephoned his own supplementary statement. Van Hamm's stenographer took it down, read his notes back to Cromwell, and that statement, too, was published by *The World*. In it Cromwell denied that any syndicate existed He said that neither he nor anyone connected with him had ever made a penny out of Panama Canal securities But he never had the alleged blackmailers indicted or tried.

In historic perspective the significant part of Cromwell's statement was. "I suppose it will be years before the beneficiaries [of the United States payment of $40,000,000] will all be identified and the distribution completely made." Who got all of the American taxpayers' $40,000,000 remained part of the untold story.

*The World* printed, in all, six articles on the incidents growing out of the Cromwell complaint. Reproduced in many newspapers across the country, they were ignored by President Theodore Roosevelt until the *Indianapolis News*, which had refused to support the Republican ticket that year, said editorially on the day before election that the American people were entitled to know "who got the money."

Humiliated politically by Taft's carrying Indiana by only 10,731 and Republicans losing the governorship and the legislature of that State, Theodore Roosevelt used the remaining four months of his Presidential term to belittle his newspaper critics. On December 1, 1908 he denounced the conduct of Delavan Smith of the *Indianapolis News* as "not merely scandalous but infamous." He called Smith "a conspicuous offender against the laws of honesty and truthfulness," occupying "the same evil eminence with such men as Mr Laffan of the *New York Sun*." He said such newspapers "habitually and continually and as a matter of business practise every form of mendacity known to man."

*The World*, up to this time, had not discussed editorially this latest Panama controversy, but the attack on Delavan Smith led the Pulitzer paper to say editorially: "The inquiry was originally *The World's* and *The World* accepts Mr. Roosevelt's challenge .. Let Congress officially answer the question, Who got the money? . . . ."

*The World* challenged the accuracy of some of the Theodore Roosevelt statements concerning distribution of the $40,000,000 T. R. immediately ordered an investigation of the French canal company's records, all of which were supposed to have been delivered according to contract to the United States Government Search by the Isthmian Canal Commission found only blueprints and engineering records. The *archives* of the bankrupt French company, which were to have been turned over as part of the property purchased by the United States, had not been delivered They might have disclosed to whom the liquidators distributed the $40,000,000

The Isthmian Canal Commission's negative report, forwarded by General Luke Wright, Secretary of War, was in President Theodore Roosevelt's hands on December 14, 1908. The following day he sent his very special message to Congress —a specimen of vitriolic language unique in American history. He said Delavan Smith and Joseph Pulitzer had libeled the people and the government of the United States and should be prosecuted as criminals — not in the State courts where they were responsible if they published a libel, but in the Federal courts.

Obedient to the President's orders, Attorney General Bonaparte obtained criminal indictments in the District of Columbia, February 17, 1909, against Joseph Pulitzer, Caleb M Van Hamm and Robert Hunt Lyman of the *New York World* and Delavan Smith and Charles R Williams, co-owners of the *Indianapolis News* They had distributed copies of their publications in the District of Columbia; therefore, contended the government lawyers, their alleged crime had been committed there rather than in the cities where their papers were issued

United States District Attorney Joseph B Kealing of Indianapolis, a Roosevelt appointee, resigned rather than be a party to such a stretching of the law. He said the order to extradite and try the Indianapolis publishers in Washington involved a dangerous principle "striking at the very foundation of our form of government"

A more pliable Federal attorney was appointed A Special Assistant United States Attorney General, Stuart McNamara, was sent to Indianapolis. Extradition proceedings, instituted in June, were ended October 15, 1909, by Federal Judge Albert B Anderson's historic decision. It closed with these words, which Theodore Roosevelt was never allowed to forget

To my mind that man has read the history of our institutions to little purpose who does not look with grave apprehension upon the possibility of the success of a proceeding such as this If the history of liberty means anything, if constitutional guarantees are worth anything, this proceeding must fail

If the prosecuting authorities have the authority to select the tribunal, if there be more than one tribunal to select from, if the government has that power and can drag citizens from distant States to the capital of the nation, there to be tried them, as Judge Cooley says, this is a strange result of a revolution where one of the grievances complained of was the assertion of the right to send parties abroad for trial The defendants will be discharged

Overlooked by historians of that decisive battle for freedom of the press was the part of Hilton U. Brown, General Manager of the *Indianapolis News* in 1909 and its Vice President until his death, September 20, 1958.

"If the spelling isn't fresh in your memory," I wrote Mr Brown, "will you please ask one of your staff to let me know whether the Federal attorney's name was 'Kealing' or "Keating,' since the old records do not agree." Mr Brown replied on September 16, 1958

I can set you right at once about the Federal attorney's name, for he was a college mate of mine. It was Joseph B Kealing He was a big stalwart man of courage and a power in politics . . . .

I was subpoenaed to deliver books and papers of *The Indianapolis News* to the Federal attorney in Washington Our astute attorneys told me to go to Washington but not to take any books. When they put me on the witness stand in Washington I said I did not bring the books as demanded because as Manager of *The News* I was an employee and had no more right to them than I had to the presses that printed the paper. I was quickly released, of course, from any further testimony.

I hope to see you in New York next year, as you suggest, but as that will be beyond my 100th year, I had better not make any assurances

February 20, 1958, was "Hilton U Brown Day" in Indianapolis, by proclamation of the Mayor Mr Brown flew into New York in April, 1958, to attend his 58th meeting of the American Newspaper Publishers Association Within a month of his death he pushed a button starting seven new presses for his newspaper, opened the new quarters of the Indianapolis Press Club, and flew to the national convention of his fraternity, Phi Delta Theta.

I had hoped to pay tribute in my Author's Preface of this book to the memory of Hilton U Brown as the other "sole survivor" of the "libel war" with T R

The government could have asked the Supreme Court to reverse Judge Anderson, but it decided to avoid, at least temporarily, the issue of extradition So it relied on an earlier indictment of the Press Publishing Company, as the corporation responsible for the alleged libel printed in Joseph Pulitzer's *New York World*, and one of its managing editors, Caleb M Van Hamm This indictment in the Federal jurisdiction of New York had been handed down on the day President William Howard Taft was inaugurated, March 4, 1909.

The New York indictment was based on the false assumption that there was a Federal libel law, and that the Federal Court had jurisdiction because *The World* had circulated 28 copies of the alleged libel "within the fort and military post and reservation of West Point" and one, for copyright purposes, had been mailed in the Federal Post Office in New York City There were then no less than 2,809 similar Federal reservations in any one of which an editor might be in jeopardy!

My recollections of the indicting procedure in New York are vivid for this reason. For several days I was held under subpoena and was threatened with contempt proceedings when I reiterated to the grand jury that, because I was preparing the defense of my newspaper on questions of fact, I would not answer any question that might disclose the line of its defense

We of *The World* were fully aware by then of ruthless espionage in support of Theodore Roosevelt's determination to destroy his critics So I stood my ground The stormy sessions ended with nothing but threats. Finally Special Assistant Attorney General Stuart McNamara whispered to me in the anteroom of the grand jury· "You needn't come back again "

The New York indictments, although finally quashed by unanimous decision of the United States Supreme Court on January 3, 1911, were pushed through in 1909, and then began the long struggle to uncover the hidden secrets of the Panama Canal scandal and the paternity of the Panama Republic

*Chapter 6*

# Who Really Got the American Taxpayer's $40,000,000

Assembling of evidence for *The World's* defense was impeded at every turn by government and Cromwell operatives. Galley proofs of articles on the Panama affair were spirited out of *The World's* composing room as quickly as duplicate sets reached editors' desks. Editors and reporters assigned to the Panama investigation were followed, their telephones tapped, their telegrams and mail intercepted.

Contrary to President Theodore Roosevelt's assertion that there was no syndicate speculating in securities of the French canal company, *The World* dug up the record of three financial groups in the United States that had functioned at various times since the beginning of the De Lesseps enterprise. This research continued long after the first Roosevelt outburst in 1908.

Unexpected by *World* editors were two breath-taking windfalls. The first came in a typewritten memorandum from John Craig Hammond, an experienced magazine and newspaper writer familiar to Wall Street and Park Row of that day. He was best known for having been press representative of the New York Central Railroad and for his contacts with Senator Chauncey M. Depew and E. H. Harriman. Hammond had been told some but apparently not all details of the widely-rumored syndicate operations and said he believed he could get documentary evidence.

Hammond told Don C Seitz, business manager of *The World*, and me on December 26, 1908 that he was working on another financial scandal story for a magazine when promised that if he would drop that investigation he would be given a much bigger story — the inside of the Panama syndicate operations He told us that he had so far only a promise of the original syndicate agreement and a record of the distribution of syndicate profits. This would not be made available, Hammond said, until March 5, 1909 and then only if release to *The World* were approved by one member of the group whose identity he was pledged to protect from publicity. The Hammond documents were in Safe No 1453 of the Nassau Bank on March 2 and from there Hammond had them delivered to *The World*, subject to that one reservation

Hammond's confidential reports to us of conferences with principals in Washington disclosed that Senator Depew was the one whose identity was to be shielded, and that the motive of Depew and Harriman, at first vindictively anti-Roosevelt, had changed when Roosevelt's term in the White House ended on March 4, 1909 Hammond told us that the urge to suppress the documents was so great that he was allowed to leave a conference in Washington only after he told his politically and financially important friends that the syndicate agreement and the bank record had been destroyed.

But the defense of the Roosevelt-instituted libel suits had to go on. So the Hammond documents were submitted to handwriting experts, who pronounced evidently genuine the signatures on the syndicate agreement and the witnessing by "WNC" as that of the easily identifiable script of William Nelson Cromwell. Identification of the handwriting in the bank book and verification of the various amounts noted on its 16 pages could not be established Secrecy had been clamped on every crevice Did any of them "get the money" — and how much?

*The World's* attorneys early decided that if the criminal libel charges were ever brought to trial on questions of fact they would subpoena those then living whose names appeared in the documents and let the court determine whether the syndicate agreement and the bank book entries were genuine — or a "plant" devised, as some skeptics suggested, to discredit any further nosing into the antecedents of the Panama Republic.

The Hammond documents were never tested in court because the prosecution of publishers and editors was ended by the unanimous decision of the United States Supreme Court on questions of law But that decision did not materialize until January 3, 1911, and preparation for defense on questions of fact had to go on with feverish speed

Evidence of other American speculation in the French canal securities was obtained from sources other than the Hammond papers These facts will come in later In retrospect the Hammond papers belong to history and I think should have their place here for whatever light they may throw on the forces and personalities that brought forth the Panama Republic

The "Memorandum of Agreement" and the bank record brought to *The World* in 1909 were in the vault of Room 214 of the old Pulitzer Building in Park Row until that great newspaper died under the hands of those whom some of the oldtimers called "the wrecking crew." Then Robert Hunt Lyman one of the managing editors who supervised much of the collection of evidence, telephoned me I had long since moved into the business world but never lost my interest in the history of Panama. Lyman said: "Records in the old Panama vault will be discarded unless we preserve them. Will you join me?" So a mass of detail, some of which was not presented to the House Committee on Foreign Affairs for its 1912 report on "The Story of Panama," was kept in fireproof warehouse vaults under joint control of Lyman and Harding until Mr. Lyman answered his final call in 1937. Then I took over, and shall preserve the Panama papers until eventually they shall go to one of the libraries that have shown a special interest in Latin American history.

Following is the complete text of what appears to have been the original signed syndicate agreement:

*MEMORANDUM OF AGREEMENT.*

W H E R E A S, J P. Morgan & Co., J. Edward Simmons, James Stillman, Isaac Seligman, Douglas Robinson, Henry W. Taft, H H Rogers, J R. Delamar, and others desire to purchase certain shares of the capital stock of the Compagnie Nouvelle Du Canal de Panama Company, at such terms, and upon such conditions as may be named by a committee of three persons to be selected from the parties to this agreement.

N O W, T H E R E F O R E, we, the undersigned, for ourselves, our administrators and assigns, in consideration of the mutuality hereof, have agreed to and with each other as follows

*FIRST*. To purchase as many shares of the capital stock of the Compagnie Nouvelle Du Canal de Panama Company as possible, at a price not exceeding twenty per cent (20%) per share, per par value of One Hundred Dollars ($100).

*SECOND* When so acquired, to place the whole of said shares of stock in the hands of the committee herein before referred to.

*THIRD*. Said stock is to be held by said committee for the benefit of the parties to this agreement, and to be disposed of at a price not less than Fifty-five (55%) per share on a basis of One Hundred Dollars ($100) par value.

The proceeds of the sale of the stock, after deducting all and any expenses in acquiring and in making the sale thereof, are to be divided pro rata among the parties to this agreement, and according to the respective amount subscribed and paid in by them for the purchase of the aforementioned stock

IN WITNESS WHEREOF, the parties hereto have set their hands and seals this Twenty-Fifth day of May, Nineteen hundred (May 25, 1900)

*In the presence of*

| | | |
|---|---|---|
| WNC | J P Morgan & Co. | (seal) |
| WNC | James Stillman | (seal) |
| WNC | I. Seligman | (seal) |
| WNC | J. Edward Simmons | (seal) |
| WNC | J. R. Delamar | (seal) |
| WNC | Vernon H Brown | (seal) |
| WNC | Geo J Gould | (seal) |
| WNC | Chauncey M Depew | (seal) |
| MNH | E. C Converse | (seal) |
| EJH | Clarence H Mackay | (seal) |
| EJH | Douglas Robinson | (seal) |
| WNC | H. H Rogers | (seal) |
| WNC | Winslow Lanier & Co. | (seal) |
| WNC | Henry W. Taft | (seal) |
| WNC | Charles R Flint | (seal) |
| WNC | Edward J. Hill | (seal) |

June 6th, 1901

The other document delivered to *The World* by Hammond was a red Morocco leather-bound book 9-1/2 x 7-1/2 inches bearing on the cover in gold letters the then-well-known name WINDSOR TRUST CO. Stamped inside, by what apparently was a rubber stamp not identical with ones in use in the bank at that time, was BANKER'S TRUST COMPANY E. C Converse, who later became head of the Bankers Trust Company, came up through the National Tube Company, one of the reorganizations put together by Cromwell.

At the top of each of sixteen pages of the bank book, all written in the same bold hand, were the names, and one or more notations of amounts in dollars and under some names notations in parenthesis. Ten of these names were among the signers of the syndicate agreement. Six were new. The listing read.

| | |
|---|---|
| J. P. Morgan & Co. | $ 433,333 |
| J. E. Simmons | 800,000 |
| Winslow Lanier & Co. | 1,333,333 |
| George J. Gould (E H H T) | 950,000 |
| J. R. Delmar (mis-spelled) | 1,333,333 |
| Chauncey M. Depew | 385,000 |
| Clarence Mackay (see NPC) | 750,000 |
| Douglas Robinson (legal See C) | 200,000 |
| Isaac Seligman (Morton T Co see C) | 1,333,333 |
| Henry W. Taft | 190,000 |

The new names not on the "Memorandum of Agreement" were.

| | |
|---|---|
| G. W. Young | 225,000 |
| F. L. Jeffries (Amador) | 190,000 |
| Nelson P. Cromwell | 1,333,333 |
| J. R. Hill | 170,000 |
| °G W Perkins | 233,000 |
| H. J Satterlee | 200,000 |

°This entry was crossed out.

The only Jeffries associated with Dr Amador in the Panama "revolution" was the American adventurer, General Herbert Ottley Jeffries, who told me in Panama and in New York that he was promised but never got anything for his part in the independence beyond his vast land grant in the Bayano River valley — where I found him in 1909. He showed me his orders from the then President Obaldia to remain away until *The World* had finished taking testimony in Panama

"Nelson P Cromwell" appeared in some press reports of Cromwell's "Americanization" scheme in 1899 When Senator Morgan asked him to identify "Nelson P.", Cromwell refused to answer

The Hill who went to Panama in 1909 to watch the taking of testimony in advance of trial of the Roosevelt charges was Cromwell's partner Edward Bruce Hill. The "J. R. Hill" was not identified.

A memorandum written in *The World's* editorial rooms dated March 10, 1909 included the following:

"The original Cromwell syndicate as formed in 1898 was substantially changed before its reorganization in 1900 and there were further changes before the signing of the syndicate agreement which was dated June 6, 1901. At least one banker refused to continue because he said it would result in a scandal ... Other original syndicators quietly dropped out when Douglas Robinson, President Roosevelt's brother-in-law, and Henry W. Taft came in. They, too, feared the scandal.... The three original banking firms which formed the old American Financial Group which got millions of dollars of profits from the De Lesseps Company continued throughout and shared as well in the successive as well as in the final profits."

Had the Rooseveltian prosecution of publishers and editors gone to trial on questions of fact, there would have been ample proof of American speculation in securities of the French canal company. A photographic copy of ledger sheets obtained by agreement between *The World's* counsel and counsel for subpoenaed witnesses in anticipation of their examination in court shows plainly today the names of participants in some of that speculation. Under the heading "PANAMA OBLIGATION, POOL ACCOUNT" were purchases and sales dated from January 1902 to February 13, 1906. (Liquidation of the French accounts was not completed until June 1908.)

Various members of the New York banking house of Kuhn, Loeb & Co., including Jacob H. Schiff and Otto H. Kahn, and members of the banking house of J. & W. Seligman & Co., including Isaac N. Seligman, were in the "Pool Account." Notable on one of the ledger sheets was this entry:

## PAUL M. WARBURG

1903

May 20  To 1250 Panama Canal New Stock  $25,966.64
             Cables  12.00

1904

Feb. 15  By 850 Panama Canal New Stock  $18,748.78
Mch. 9  By 400 Panama Canal New Stock  8,854.97

Paul M. Warburg was the father of James P. Warburg, who began in September, 1956 campaigning for internationalization of the Panama Canal

But this proof of the existence of speculation in French canal company securities was not available when *The World's* counsel decided to send rogatory commissions to Paris and to Panama to obtain testimony in advance of trial. This was a very costly operation because the Federal Government required the defendant newspaper to pay its own and the travel and living expenses of two Federal attorneys to Paris through hearings that extended from July 20 to July 30, 1909.

The Panama expedition, with expenses of one Federal attorney charged to *The World,* was more productive because, as one disgusted operative for the prosecution was heard to remark in Panama, "Cromwell's man here was an ass and left too much evidence uncovered." But in Paris the coverup was almost complete.

The prosecution charged in the indictments that $40,000,000 had been paid through J P. Morgan & Co to the liquidators of the old and the new French canal companies. The indictments said that records of the liquidators were intact and "show the individual distribution to the individual claimants, the amounts, the dates and the residences of the persons to whom paid."

That looked easy. *The World* retained the ablest corporation lawyers in London and Paris to assist its counsel from New York. But the records of the liquidators had been sealed, and under French law must remain in the depository for ten or twenty years. Every effort to obtain access to them was frustrated. Equally futile were later requests, during the Woodrow Wilson Administration, for canal company *"archives"* which Uncle Sam had purchased. Engineering records and blueprints were delivered, but never any record of the liquidation, no proof of payment of American taxpayers' money to holders of the bonds of the old or stock of the new company, or the identity of those who had bought some of those securities in the open market before the payoff.

*The World's* British counsel, an eminent member of Parliament, reported after his search in Paris.

I have never known in my lengthy experience in company matters any public corporation, much less one of such vast importance, having so completely disappeared and removed all trace of its existence as the New Panama Canal Company The American Ambassador in Paris was entitled to the archives of the company for his government, and those archives should include a list of the persons who received the purchase money paid by the United States.

Nevertheless the Paris hearings got into the record verification of the text of the Cromwell brief — *The World* called it "Cromwell's confession" — of which one copy had grown up mysteriously over night on the desk of a Pulitzer editor Part of my research was to prove the authenticity of that windfall document — some 65,000 words in French. Finally I found Maurice Leon, a French lawyer in Wall Street, who had made the translation for Cromwell from his original English *The World* learned that only 25 copies of the French version had been printed, and that all but two had been destroyed after the French arbitrators in Paris on December 23, 1907 cut Cromwell's bill for fees and disbursements from $832,449 38 to $228,282.71. But *The World* never established the identity nor the motive of the individual who delivered to it the one "lost" or next-to-last French copy of the telltale brief.

Testimony before *The World's* rogatory commission in

Paris also proved that shares of the New Panama Canal Company sold as low as 65 in the Paris market; that control had at one time been pooled by French bankers, and that whoever held title to them until the final liquidation in June, 1908 received 129.78 per cent of their original par value.

Maurice Hutin, former president of the French company, answering a question of counsel as to whether there had been speculation in the stock, replied: "I have no doubt there were people on the Stock Exchange intelligent enough to have made such a fruitful transaction."

United States District Attorney Henry A Wise of New York and Special Assistant Attorney General Stuart McNamara hammered hard in the Paris hearing to clear the names of Douglas Robinson and others whose names had been in the stories of alleged syndicate speculation Nevertheless cross examination by *The World's* counsel established Douglas Robinson's association with some of the syndicate promoters, and subsequent proceedings revealed much more

When the libel prosecution came to a hearing in the United States Circuit Court in New York City January 24, 1910 it was disclosed that President Theodore Roosevelt's brother-in-law, Douglas Robinson, was interested in the real estate business. This was established when Judge Charles M Hough excused Edward J Roberts, a real estate appraiser for the McVickar Realty Company, after Roberts testified. "I think I ought to explain that we have had business relations with Douglas Robinson, with Mr. Cromwell and with Charles Brown, and have handled Panama funds and expect to handle more. We have placed a lot of Panama bonds."

The "Panama funds" were part of the $10,000,000 paid to the Republic of Panama by the United States. Cromwell was already Panama's fiscal agent and controlled the investment of $6,000,000 of that fund in mortgages on New York City real estate. Douglas Robinson's real estate firm passed on the applications of borrowers and the valuation of their properties

While John D. Lindsay of *The World's* counsel was preparing for the Paris expedition I was asked to provide Thomas S. Fuller, another of *The World's* counsel, with ammunition for examination of witnesses in Panama. Fuller proceeded on the assumption that the Panama conspirators, put under oath, would tell the whole truth about the "revolution."

Early in 1909 *The World* had dispatched two trusted men, Gus C Roeder of the New York staff and Harry L. Dunlap of its Washington bureau to dig in Panama. Roeder saw Dr. Amador in February, but found him ill and weak. Roeder's draft of what Amador told him was read by Ricardo Arias, who wrote that when he was "more at ease" the first President of Panama intended to "narrate all those events with perfect exactness" and would deliver his memoirs to his friends. It was apparent in February that Amador was nearing the end, which came on May 2, 1909

Roeder's only important discovery was the progress of a plan for a $400,000,000 timberland concession in which Cromwell's press agents, Farnham and Whitley, were the fronts. In Panama it was suspected that Cromwell was the principal because Farnham was known in Panama as "Cromwell's man." Farnham had engineered the concession almost through the Panama legislature before public denunciation of the project as a "steal" caused it to be quietly put asleep.

Some factions in Panama were already critical of Cromwell's handling of the loan fund. In November, 1910 six of the twenty-eight members of the Panama Assembly demanded that Cromwell be bonded, but the Assembly refused to turn against the Republic's benefactor. Instead, it adopted unanimously a resolution raising to the rank of *Hero of the Republic* Cromwell's recently-deceased adjutant, Colonel James R. Shaler, Superintendent of the Panama Railroad at the time of the "revolution."

Part of my research in New York had been directed into the background of the Amador family. Dr. Amador's son, Raoul A Amador, had been Panama's first Consul General in New York, from 1903 to 1907. He had been educated in Columbia University School of Medicine in New York and had served with distinction as an assistant surgeon in the United States Army, first in Cuba, and then at Fort Revere, Massachusetts. Why had he been replaced as Consul General?

Newspaper "morgues" bulged with clippings about Don Raoul's love life with Mrs. Bertha Kennard Gresham. The *New York Journal* had described her as a social favorite in Washington than whom "no prettier woman ever graced a state function." She was the daughter of William Edward Kennard of Washington Her first husband, Rear Admiral Frisbee, and her second, Navy Lieutenant William Gresham, had died before she was 30. A social junket to Panama brought her at the age of 32 into the embrace of the equally attractive and dashing young Dr Amador

Soon after Bertha Gresham's return from the tropics she and the Consul General were known at 306 West 87th Street in New York City as "Mr and Mrs. R. A d'Armand " The official residence of Dr. R. A. Amador and his American-born wife, Jenny Smith Amador, and their two young children was 216 West 112th Street, a house which young Dr. Amador acquired from Selma E. Sack on October 13, 1902 The 112th Street house was deeded by Raoul and Jenny Amador in May and July, 1906 to Luke H. Cutter, a clerk in Cromwell's office, and later deeded by Cutter to Manuel A Guerrero.

By October, 1906 Don Raoul's ardor for the attractive widow had cooled She upbraided him as he drove by on Riverside Drive where she was walking. The press reported that Consul General Amador pointed his buggy-whip so menacingly that on October 2, 1906 Bertha Gresham had him arrested and filed suit for $100,000, charging that young Dr. Amador was the father of her girl baby. The case was settled out of court.

"There was a romance, of course," said Consul General Amador in an interview which *The World* published on October 5, 1906. "I'm not given to denying palpable facts, especially when a lady sees fit to make them public. But it was not the case of a man of the world wronging an ingenue. Mrs. Gresham has been twice widowed. I think it was a situation in which both understood ourselves thoroughly. I was married and she knew it. The day arrived when I said adieu.... She tried coercion I told her to go as far as she liked."

More investigation convinced me that old Dr. Amador dearly loved his son Raoul —much more than he loved Raoul's half-brother Manuel, who had succeeded Raoul as Consul General. It became evident that Raoul, or his mother, Maria de la Ossa de Amador, would have whatever confidential papers the first President of Panama had not destroyed. With the cabled news that old Dr Amador had died on May 2, 1909, Don Raoul became, to my mind, the most valuable witness in Panama I had heard the Spanish adage, *el papel se rompe el* — let the paper destroy itself — but its full significance was not impressed upon me until later, in Panama.

I went to the Panama liner on which our rogatory commission was embarking June 3, 1909 and handed to Fuller a memorandum on the background of possible witnesses that could, if they would, tell the whole truth about the Panama "revolution." I stressed the importance of Raoul Amador Fuller seemed not impressed. But the presence aboard of Cromwell's law partner, Edward B. Hill, accompanying Assistant United States District Attorney James R Knapp, was to me sufficient warning. Every bit of telltale evidence in Panama would be bottled up.

It was three in the afternoon. I hurried back to *The World*, told my misgivings to Don Seitz, and instantly got his clearance to take the next train for New Orleans, leaving New York at 4:30 P. M. A United Fruiter from that port would land me in Panama a day or two after our rogatory commission would arrive from New York. I arrived at the Hotel Tivoli, Canal Zone, at noon of June 11 and spent that evening in conference with Fuller.

One must follow, at least briefly, the sequence of developments from this point to see how nearly the story of Panama escaped being told.

*Chapter 7*

# Amador's "Dear Little Son" Held History's Key

Taking of testimony by *The World's* rogatory commission in the court of Panamanian Judge Hector Valdez began June 11, 1909 I arrived, via New Orleans, at noon of that day and spent the evening in conference with Fuller. Before starting the hearings Fuller had talked with the surviving members of the Revolutionary Junta. Amador and Arango had died within a few days of each other. Only Federico Boyd, Ricardo Arias, Tomas Arias and Amador's brother-in-law, Manuel Espinosa B., were still available

According to Boyd's sworn testimony on June 14, 1909 there were only "four principals" in the original junta of eight Panamanian patriots — "Amador, Arango, [Ricardo] Arias and myself Those are the ones that got up all the work." Boyd swore that not more than 50 persons in Panama knew of the revolutionary plan until the day of the independence. That was how, as President Theodore Roosevelt assured a news-hungry world, the people of Panama rose literally as one man!

Fuller shocked me with his first statement that evening. He said the "founding fathers" had all told him substantially the same story. There had been no collusive understanding with the government in Washington. The Panama affair had been all that T R had assured Congress and the American people it had been — "as clean as a hound's tooth "

Then Fuller nearly bowled me over with this. "*The World* has been misled, we haven't a leg to stand on."

"What about young Amador?" I asked.

Without a trace of disbelief in his voice Fuller replied: "They all tell me his father called young Amador *loco* and didn't trust him with anything. The bad publicity about him in New York would discredit our case if we used him as a witness We must have nothing to do with him."

The taking of testimony before Judge Hector Valdez continued from June 11 to June 19. The court permitted witnesses, under Panamanian procedure, to amend their testimony before completing the record. We learned later that if the record of the rogatory hearings in Panama, with its astounding documents, had been presented in New York it was to be thrown out under a technicality of Panamanian law, and that Boyd and Arias would be there to testify in person.

Throughout the rogatory hearings Cromwell's partner, Edward B Hill, sat at the elbow of United States Attorney Knapp The pressure on witnesses was obvious. Knapp sprinkled the record with objections to Fuller's questions. Only over objections was *The World's* associate counsel, Dr. Oscar Teran, a Panamanian still loyal to his mother country Colombia, permitted to be present when files of the Central and South American Telegraph Company were searched for copies of messages from Cromwell, Amador, Bunau-Varilla and others deep in the "revolution." The 372 pages of testimony taken in the rogatory hearings in Panama — which I have just re-read — were filled with legal sparring before it was put in the record that all of the telltale cable messages had been conveniently — of course inadvertently — destroyed!

Ricardo and Tomas Arias, Manuel Espinosa B. and Federico Boyd told mixed and conflicting stories about the planning, the financing and execution of the "revolution." Fortunately we had the text of Arango's unexpurgated *"Data for a History of the Independence"* and the New York hotel and steamship records of Amador's and Boyd's movements when Amador and Boyd waited over in New York, November 17-18, 1903, to keep the appointment that Cromwell's brief said had been arranged at their request. Boyd swore that he and Amador didn't see Cromwell until later in Washington. Confronted by the records, Boyd said the hotel and steamship records must have been incorrect.

The Ariases and Espinosa and Jose Augustin Arango Jr., who was called to testify for his deceased father, added only confusion to the story They wouldn't admit knowledge of Arango's having — as he wrote in his history — sought out Captain James R Beers and sent him on the "delecate mission" to enlist Cromwell's advice and help They swore that no financing was arranged before the "revolution" but no two stories agreed as to what part was played by Bunau-Varilla, J P Morgan & Co. and the Bowling Green Trust Company and various Panamanians in providing funds. Boyd said that he and President Amador signed for a $100,-000 loan at the Bowling Green Trust Company on November 25, 1903 but that he knew nothing of Cromwell's having deposited $90,000 of Union Pacific and $10,000 of Baltimore & Ohio bonds to guarantee that loan.

While this record, largely confirming Fuller's earlier fears that defeat was in store for us, was being built up in court, between June 11 and June 15, I was quietly cultivating Raoul Amador. There was no time to consult *World* headquarters even if cables had been safe. I had to act on my own responsibility in disobeying our attorney's orders to have nothing to do with young Amador.

Don Raoul was friendly, and several times he said he

would let me see his father's *archivos,* but each day he had some excuse I had not yet discovered the key to his mind.

On the day Fuller discovered in court that the all-important cable evidence had been destroyed, I was waiting in the cafe of the Hotel Central for Don Raoul. He was coming this time, he assured me, so that I might have "at least the satisfaction of being able to say I had seen the Amador archives "

Waiting an hour past our appointment became unbearable. I started for the Amador country home, met Don Raoul en route, dismissed my *cochero* and came back to the Central in the Amador family carriage Meanwhile I had learned much about Panamanian political antipathies. Jealousies, bitterness and distrust were a common heritage of the "revolution " Who had double-crossed whom? Who got how much out of it? What became of the first million of the $10,000,000 from the United States? Nobody could, or would, tell.

I reminded Don Raoul that this was nearly our last day, Federal Attorney Knapp, in his role of prosecutor, was about to take over the hearings before Judge Hector Valdez Must our rogatory commission be denied the right to see what Don Raoul's father had left for history?

Apologetically Don Raoul exclaimed to me. "I'm so sorry! I forgot! I left the key to our town house in the country!"

I had been forced to plan the next step With indignation in my voice I said "Don Raoul, I'm sorry, too — for I'm forced to the conclusion that you've been filling me with plain North American bull!" (He used *yanqui* slang like a North American ) Naming one of the Junta with whom I had learned that young Amador was not on friendly terms, I said "Don So-and-So ought to know — and he's authority for the statement that your father thought you were *loco,* never had any confidence in you, and never trusted you with anything!"

Don Raoul hit the ceiling with Spanish expletives. "You come over to my house! I'll show you whether my father had confidence in me!"

## Amador's "Dear Little Son" Held History's Key

"How'll you get in without a key?"

"Come with me, I'll show you!"

A walk around the corner brought us to the Amador town home, and a thrust of Don Raoul's shoulder pushed the tropically light wooden door past its lock Reaching up for a hidden key, he unlocked a battered old steamer trunk and from its lower right-hand corner pulled a packet of letters tied in red ribbon. He untied, I watched.

"So they say my father didn't trust me! Read this letter!"

Addressed to "Dear Little Son," the letter, perfectly preserved, was in old Dr Amador's careful script. Don Raoul told me that his father wrote the letter in New York two days before he sailed for Panama to carry out the agreed plans for the "revolution," and that he, Don Raoul, received it in the mail at Fort Revere, Massachusetts.

The "Dear Little Son" letter contradicted the stories which the "founding fathers" had been telling before our rogatory commission. It showed that the United States Government would prevent Colombia from landing troops to put down a revolt Only the Canal Zone would be declared independent and brought under the immediate protection of the United States The other districts of the Isthmus would be brought in later — as they were — and "these also will be under the protection of the United States." A Minister would be on hand — as Bunau-Varilla was, in Washington —"to take up the treaty In 30 days everything will be concluded." Financing of the "revolution," Dr. Amador assured his son, "already has been arranged with a bank"

As Don Raoul finished reading the letter, translating his father's Spanish into fluent English, he turned to me.

"Isn't that just what your newspaper has been trying to prove?"

It was Would he let me place the letter in the court record? Without hestiation he said yes.

By this time we knew how evidence could disappear. Taking no chances, I had the precious letter photographed that afternoon, dispatched plates and prints of it by the last train to Colon for mail to New York, and then showed the original to Fuller. His objection to using Don Raoul as a witness was partially withdrawn, but he still would try to avoid any extensive cross-examination. United States Attorney Knapp didn't ask Don Raoul a single question.

Some alert historians — not Panamanians — picked up the "Dear Little Son" letter after it was read into the record of the Congressional investigation under the Rainey resolution on February 13, 1912 But the story of how it escaped destruction along with other records of the "revolution" is printed here for the first time.

Another memento of historic value given to me by Don Raoul was his carefully-preserved souvenir program of the luncheon he gave in the Waldorf-Astoria February 20, 1904 — the day his father was inaugurated in Panama as the First President of the Republic. This limited social function was tendered to those men in New York who had done most to help the independence and to whom President Amador and his son wished to show appreciation. Under the photograph of President Amador — the best picture of him I have ever seen — was printed the guest list, so arranged, out of alphebetical order, that their relative importance seems obvious
William Nelson Cromwell
Geo. H. Sullivan
E. B. Hill
William J Curtis
R. L Farnham

E. A Drake
Charles Paine
R L. Walker
S. Deming
Mr. M J. Echeverria

After Cromwell were listed his three senior partners and his press agent; then Drake, Paine, Walker and Deming, all Panama Railroad men. The only Panamanian guest, Dr. Echeverria, was a physician living in New York. Before this souvenir was introduced in the rogatory commission's hearings the patriots had testified that the "revolution" received no assistance from Panama Railroad officials or employees — the assistance that made possible their Republic!

Besides the luncheon record of Panama's obligation to Cromwell and his partners and to Panama Railroad men, Don Raoul gave me another item, a manuscript. A photographic copy is in front of me. The original text covered fourteen note-paper-size sheets, all in old Dr. Amador's clear Spanish script. He had crossed out some whole paragraphs, interlined others and corrected words and phrases — all in his unmistakable hand. Fuller had Don Raoul identify both the letter and the manuscript. Photographic copies of both documents were made part of the rogatory commission's record.

But the manuscript told only such parts of the story of the "revolution" as old Dr. Amador wished posterity to know. His mental reservations — details which he knew and carried to his grave — are for another chapter.

*Chapter 8*

# Panamanians Learn Early the Art of Political Blackmail

Dr Amador's mental reservations when he wrote out in longhand his history of the "revolution" were best known, and perhaps known *only*, to these three.

Maria de la Ossa de Amador, devoted and resolute wife of Panama's first President, their son, Don Raoul A. Amador, and Dona Maria's brother, Francisco de la Ossa, for many years Alcalde (Mayor) of the City of Panama.

During the month that I stayed on in Panama after *The World's* rogatory commission closed its obstructed hearings in June, 1909, facts which eluded the lawyers' search, secret codes and hidden messages, came to me from unexpected sources Many doors were opened by Henry N. Hall, then editor of the English section of the daily newspaper owned by men in the Panama Government. Hall later joined *The World's* staff and in February, 1912, presented much, but by no means all, of the untold story of Panama to the House Committee on Foreign Affairs in Washington.

More immediately helpful was Dr. Oscar Teran, associate counsel for *The World* in Panama, able lawyer, formerly a member of the Colombian Congress and loyal to his mother country. Dr. Teran knew the procedures under Panamanian law to obtain for me access to government accounts.

Most helpful of all was Don Raoul Amador, who introduced me to his mother's brother. My day-to-day notes, which I preserved, recorded eight luncheon, dinner and other meetings I had with Don Raoul or with Don Francisco de la Ossa or both, between June 27 and July 15, 1909. This friendly contact was renewed when I returned to Panama to gather still more facts in 1910, and was continued in correspondence after Don Raoul withdrew from the turmoil of Panamanian politics in the spring of 1911 before he settled down in Paris, where he and his mother made their home for many years.

My memoranda fix a luncheon date with Senor de la Ossa at the Canal Zone's Hotel Tivoli as June 28, 1909, when he told me.

Panamanians are afraid to tell the truth that the revolution was hatched in New York. About eight days before the revolution my sister made me swear on the photograph of our deceased mother that I would not tell anyone what I had heard, and that as Alcalde of what was then a Colombian city I would take no action against my friends.

Don Francisco was true to his family ties. We had lunch again on July 4, saw each other briefly in the Hotel Central on the 9th, and in a conversation lasting from 2:30 to 4 P. M. on July 10 he told me in some detail the extent of the Amador estate, which included small holdings of Panama real estate. I saw Don Francisco again on July 13, at 3:30 P. M., when he told me that the surviving members of the Revolutionary Junta were bullying his sister, demanding that she tell nóthing to *The World* man because they were afraid, if she told all she knew, she would make them out liars. They said she was "only a woman, and knew nothing about the revolution."

Don Francisco told me he resented their aspersions, because "everybody, including Herbert Prescott, knows that Dona Maria had more nerve than all the men and did more than anyone else to keep the conspiracy from falling through."

Prescott, whom I came to know very well after he testified before our rogatory commission on June 15, 1909, confirmed to me the de la Ossa estimate of Dona Maria's part in saving the "revolution" from disaster. On my return to Panama in 1910 to gather up evidence which had evaded our rogatory commission's search, Prescott permitted me to copy from his file of revolutionary treasures the grandiose cable from Cromwell about presenting the first flag of Panama to President Theodore Roosevelt. From Prescott's files I was permitted to find leads to other undestroyed documents, also to take photographic copy of a three-page letter Cromwell wrote in his own hand to Prescott on March 14, 1905, telling Prescott to work with John F. Wallace, who was chief engineer of Panama Canal construction from 1904 until June 28, 1905.

Maria de la Ossa de Amador's commanding influence in saving the "revolution" became a legend in Latin America. It was so widely known that in 1926 a responsible businessman, one of the hosts of a social gathering in Havana, Cuba, said to my wife when she happened to mention Panama, "Of course you know Amador's wife ordered the old man to get out of his hammock and go back to the barracks and see the revolution through."

The prevalent story in Panama was that Dr. Amador was terrified and went home to his wife after the one Colombian gunboat in Panama harbor, whose captain hadn't been bribed, fired into the city the shells that inflicted the only casualties of the War of Independence — one Chinese and one donkey.

Naturally the "founding fathers" were disturbed when Dr. Amador's letter to his "Dear Little Son" Raoul was read into the rogatory commission's record. Privately, the patriots upbraided Don Raoul for having told some of their secrets. They proceeded to make his political life in Panama miserable until he took himself away in 1911 to Kingston, Jamaica, and to Paris where he died March 23, 1934. Publicly, to explain their own contradictory testimony, the patriots declared that old Dr. Amador never told them the whole truth. Nor did he. Here is his son's explanation, as told to me by Don Raoul himself and written down by me at the time.

My father told me before his death that Panama will some day need the friendship of the American government, and that for this reason he would never tell all he knew about the revolution. Father put it this way. "If the American Government finds out that we do not keep our political secrets, it will no longer trust us."

Countless discrepancies between fact and fiction in Panamanian history and proofs of the patriots' frantic efforts to cover up evidence kept coming to the surface. Here are a few examples·

When it became known in July, 1909, that I was going to Bogota to check up on the patriots' testimony, Federico Boyd's brother, Samuel Boyd, approached Edwin Warren Guyol, a New Orleans-born roving magazine writer whose knowledge of Isthmian affairs had been useful to me. Would Guyol report confidentially to Boyd on Harding's activities? With my approval, Guyol conferred at length with Sam Boyd and they signed up an agreement on July 15.

Sam Boyd then prepared a private cable code covering more than 100 names and possible developments. Guyol was to impede my contacts with Bogota officials and cooperate with a French wine salesman, the Marquis Alexander de Ste. Croix, who was going to Bogota ahead of me. Ste. Croix's closeness to United States Attorney Knapp and Cromwell's partner Hill during the rogatory commission's sessions in Panama justified the suspicion that wine salesmanship was a cover for secret service work Ste Croix spent most of his time in Bogota in the American Legation. He was very busy in Bogota advising Colombian government officials to tell nothing to Harding Nevertheless, they gave me certified copies of all cables between Bogota and Washington which later enabled *The World* to show that many had been withheld when President Roosevelt told Congress he had transmitted *all* of the official correspondence on the Panama controversy.

Sam Boyd was an early Director of Posts and Telegraphs of the Republic of Panama and in 1909 was the *New York Herald's* correspondent there. Boyd was to pay Guyol's tolls and out-of-pocket expenses in relaying information. Boyd, over his own signature, wrote:

"It is further understood that I will personally undertake to arrange with the gentlemen in New York and Panama who are interested in obtaining the information in question, for proper compensation, and that whatever amount they appropriate for the service shall be equally divided between you [Guyol] and myself."

The patriots testified that the Bogota government left its garrison in Panama unpaid for so long that it was easy to bribe General Esteban Huertas and his officers I found this was untrue, for in Bogota I obtained certified copies of Treasury accounts showing that drafts covering troop payrolls for Panama had been forwarded every month and receipted by the commandant in Panama

When we wanted General Huertas's testimony before the rogatory commission we found that he had been ordered away "somewhere in the interior." The same with General Herbert Ottley Jeffries, American adventurer, whom I found on his 200,000-acre timberland concession up the Bayano River The land grant was part of Jeffries' reward for his scheduled part as "admiral" of whatever Colombian guncraft the Junta might capture.

Another much-wanted witness was Dr. Eusebio A. Morales, then Minister of Public Instruction. President Obaldia had instructed him to extend his inspection of rural schools. I waited in Panama until he returned.

Dr. Oscar Teran drafted my questions to Dr. Morales in such form that a Cabinet Minister, although he could not be subpoenaed under Panamanian law, must answer. Dr. Morales' written replies, dated June 29, 1909, were courteous and explicit, his oral amplifications still more illuminating

President Theodore Roosevelt's campaign for re-election was at its height in September, 1904, when Dr. Morales began giving to United States newspapers statements critical of the American government's interpretation of the Hay-Bunau-Varilla Treaty of 1903. Controversies involved tariff rates and jurisdiction over the ports of Panama and Colon.

We knew that Dr. Morales had written an article for the *North American Review*, "The Panama Canal Treaty, Its History and Interpretation " Why had he withdrawn it?

Dr. Morales replied that "some distinguished persons were at my hotel to beg of me not to publish the article, thinking doubtless that it might contain revelations against President Roosevelt's connection with the independence of Panama."

(This was seven years and five months before T. R. boasted that he "took the Isthmus and left Congress to debate ")

The "distinguished persons," Dr Morales later told me orally, were two men speaking for the Treasurer of the Republican National Committee They expressed to him fear that the Panama story, if told then, might cause T. R. to lose the election, so they offered to reimburse Dr. Morales for whatever the *North American Review* would pay for his article if he would withdraw it He told me he would not accept their offered compensation, but did write to the editor to kill his article the day after President Roosevelt "addressed to Secretary Taft the celebrated letter in which he gave the latter instructions to come to Panama and effect a settlement of the pending questions."

"Happily for Panama President Roosevelt convinced himself of the justice of our claims...." so "the publication [of his article] no longer had any object." This is from Dr. Morales' written reply to me.

Following T.R.'s triumphant re-election, Secretary of War William Howard Taft (four years later to be President), accompanied by Panama's fiscal agent and general counsel, William Nelson Cromwell, went to Panama. They were photographed arm-in-arm. Secretary Taft gave the Panamanian politicians what they wanted. Both he and Cromwell spoke at a grand banquet in the Hotel Central, December 1, 1904, and Cromwell on December 29 was made an *hijo benemerito* (meritorious son) of the Republic.

Thus, very early in their experience, Panamanian politicians learned how and when to apply pressure. The "founding fathers" taught their sons, who, through the years, have become adept in the practice of getting what they want from Uncle Sam.

*Chapter 9*

# *Amador Got His Assurance Direct From T. R.*

My second fact-hunting expedition in 1910 was more productive than our rogatory commission's hearings in 1909 partly because factional political turmoil was boiling up in Panama's presidential campaign. Ernesto LeFevre was upbraiding Don Raoul Amador for having given me in 1909 the "Dear Little Son" letter and the sciipt that old Dr. Amador had written and edited carefully to leave still untold much of the real story of Panama. Such internal bickering opened unexpected doors.

One of the several windfalls was the changed attitude of Don Tomas Arias. He permitted me to copy from his record book the full text of the private codes used by old Dr. Amador and Arango, Joshua Lindo and Bunau-Varilla. The long-hidden codes and Arango's letter to Dr. Amador in New York —which Amador was asked to destroy but didn't— tore apart the veil of deceit that had shrouded the "revolution."

Another windfall was the friendly attitude of *The Panama Journal,* a Government organ On its front page, March 22, 1910, under a two-column heading, "Personal Mention of People," *The Journal* said:

> Mr Earl Harding, one of the many capable newspaper men connected with the great *New York World,* and who has been in Panama for several weeks seeking information for that paper in the matter of the libel suit brought by the United States against the proprietor, will leave on the Royal Mail for New York, having secured the information he sought
>
> During Mr Harding's visit on the Isthmus he has made many friends by his genial, affable and obliging manners, all of whom will wish him success wherever his duties may call him, and assure him of a hearty welcome whenever he chooses to make Panama another visit.

Don Raoul Amador was being falsely accused of having given me the telltale Arango letter. It came from an entirely different source I still have the photographic copy of Arango's Spanish script. It gives the positive lie to the patriots' story that old Dr Amador cabled "Disappointed" after Cromwell turned him down, and then cabled "Hopes" after Bunau-Varilla assured him of military and financial support for the "revolution." The Arango letter, clearly dated September 14, 1903, shows that both of these messages were sent before Dr Amador ever met Bunau-Varilla, who did not arrive in New York until September 22, 1903.

On my 1910 sojourn in Panama Don Raoul Amador and I became so well acquainted that he finally told me he would like to be appointed *The World's* official correspondent — not for the modest compensation, which he said he did not need, but because all other news channels on the Isthmus were controlled by politicians then in power. Sam Boyd was correspondent of the *New York Herald* and Ernesto Le-Fevre covered the *Associated Press.*

Don Raoul cabled some news, and wrote me in personal letters in April, June and July, 1910, more complete reports of the political turmoil. Then I heard no more except in brief news cables, until he wrote me from Kingston, Jamaica, April 30, 1911. In part he said·

I am glad I am out of it . I have been doing nothing but taking care of my animals, my four dogs and my horse, which I brought with me, and that keeps me busy . My mother is in Europe and will not return until October, so I guess I am a fixture here till then. Do drop me a line With best regards, believe me as ever,
Sincerely yours,

R.A A

When I last saw Don Raoul in Panama in March, 1910, I told him we expected the criminal libel prosecution would come to trial in New York, and in that event we would need his testimony He told me he would, if subpoenaed, tell the truth as his father had confided it to him before his death—

That Dr Amador would take no one's word, neither Cromwell's nor Bunau-Varilla's, but went himself to Washington

That Dr. Amador arrived in Washington late in the evening went to the White House, talked late with President Theodore Roosevelt, and returned to New York on an early morning train to avoid being seen in any hotel.

(This was the coverup technique Farnham had used to conceal J. Gabriel Duque's visit to the capital in 1903.)

Senator Morgan of Alabama heard when he started his investigation of the "revolution" that Dr Amador had paid a night visit to the White House, but had never been able to verify that information.

Still further, Don Raoul said to me:

Father told me he did not dare risk his life and the

lives of our people on any second-hand promises. Roosevelt put Father into a cab at the White House, placed his hand on Father's shoulder, and said:

"Go ahead, Doctor, we'll see you through."

Naturally, *The World,* preparing for trial on questions of both law and fact, sought confirmation of the evidence we now felt certain Don Raoul Amador would repeat and perhaps amplify in court.

Don Raoul told me in 1909 that his father had confided his revolutionary plans to Robert B. Alling, a New York lawyer whose wife was a sister of Don Raoul's American wife, Jenny Smith Amador. Alling confirmed this in an interview with a *World* reporter in his law office, 1102 Singer Building, September 11, 1909. He said he told the Amadors not to take seriously any promises of help from Washington.

Still more direct information came from an unexpected source — Wall Street. S. S. Fontaine, financial editor of *The World,* sent to Don Seitz this memorandum

"Dr. Philip Embury of 250 West 70th Street was a chum of the son of President Amador of Panama when he was a student at Columbia Dr Embury told a Wall Street friend of mine recently that young Amador said to him about two weeks before the Panama revolution

" 'Look out for a shakeup in Panama in a few days. The Old Man has been down to see Roosevelt and Hay, and he's got the money and backing to pull the thing off."

Seitz sent a trusted reporter from whose memorandum, dated November 17, 1910, 8 30 P M , I quote.

"Called by appointment on Dr. Philip Embury, 250 West 70th St., at five-thirty this afternoon, showed him statement from Mr. Fontaine and asked him to confirm it. After reading it through he made statements substantially in the following words.

"Yes, this is perfectly true. You see, I knew Raoul very well What actually happened with Raoul was this.

"He came here one evening in October 1903 in a new

automobile. When I teased Raoul about not having been around before in his new car he said that he had been too busy going about with his father; that the 'old man' was here on important business connected with Panama; that *together* they had been to Washington, had seen and conferred with Roosevelt and John Hay, and after their return to New York his father sailed for Panama with all arrangements completed, that within three weeks we could expect to hear of a red hot revolution down in Panama, as we certainly did

"Raoul walked up and down this office like a caged bear the whole time that he was talking... Did Raoul tell you about the way a man named Beers was sent up here, before old Amador came North, to arrange the preliminaries? The thing was cut and dried."

The reporter's memorandum added· "Dr. Embury is about 35 or 36 years old, evidently has money and a good practice, is very deliberate in manner; spoke without effort or hesitation, made flat statements, unqualified, excepting that he was not certain of the name of the banker mentioned by Raoul Amador."

Mrs. Bertha Gresham, Don Raoul's one-time enamorita told me on June 16, 1910, that while she and young Amador were living together in West 87th Street, New York, he told her repeatedly of his having been with his father in a midnight conference in the White House, and of President Theodore Roosevelt's having told Dr Amador that the Panamanians could depend upon the United States to see them through

It was generally known that Dr Amador visited his son at Fort Revere, Massachusetts, but their later movements were kept a dark secret. Don Raoul told me he was so sure of the outcome that he tendered his resignation in advance as assistant surgeon in the United States Army and, without leave, came to New York to watch newspaper bulletin boards on November 3 for the news he knew was coming.

For more than 20 years Don Raoul and his mother made

their home in Paris until his death on March 23, 1934. Panamanian politicians who condemned him in 1909 for his truth-telling "indiscretion" before our rogatory commission came to appreciate his sparkling personality and his loyalty to his native country. He served Panama in Paris in various capacities, up to the rank of Minister to France. His second wife, the former Marthe Lenoir, and his mother, Maria de la Ossa de Amador, were with him in his brief final illness. After 1939 his mother made her last home with her daughter, Mrs Elmira Ehrman, in Charlottesville, North Carolina, where she died on July 5, 1948, at the age of 93

*Chapter 10*

# *Coverups and Contradictions*

To cover up telltale evidence and conceal the sources of opulence sprouting in the private lives of some of the Panama patriots as well as in the purses of bribed Colombian soldiers and generals a technique was used which was calculated to make detection difficult

Law 48 of 1904, passed by the Panama National Assembly and signed on May 13, 1904, by President Amador, legalized in lump sum all expenditures of the infant Republic up to and including June 30, 1904. They footed up to $3,000,000 Panamanian silver, equal at the then rate of exchange to $1,365,000 U.S gold J Gabriel Duque, proprietor of the lottery and of the *Panama Star & Herald*, told me in Panama that accounts showing the distribution of this money had been burned by agreement in a secret session of the National Assembly

The juggling of funds, the use of cash from the sale of the Panama Railroad to bribe Colombian soldiers, and the conflicting accounts of temporary loans by Panamanian businessmen are a long, involved story. The whole truth will probably never be told. Most of the facts were buried, as I found later, by the legalized lump-sum accounting under Law 48 of 1904. I did not obtain access to the record of that blind accounting until after our rogatory commission had departed

According to Bunau-Varilla, the preliminary financing of the "revolution" was arranged this way. On October 22, 1903, Bunau-Varilla cabled his bankers to remit to him in New York $100,000 Cromwell arrived in Paris on October 23, 1903, and Bunau-Varilla's bankers established the $100,000 credit in New York on October 26 Was this by coincidence? Or was it prearranged — and by whom?

This much is conceded. Bunau-Varilla forced his own appointment as Panama's first Envoy Extraordinary and Minister Plenipotentiary over the vehement objection of Dr. Amador, whose early distrust of the Frenchman was inherited by his son Raoul — as Don Raoul frankly told me in 1910

Bunau-Varilla's rush to sign the Hay-Bunau-Varilla Treaty has never been forgiven by Panamanians They never liked the treaty Dr. Amador and Federico Boyd, as special commissioners from the Junta in Panama, as told in Chapter IV, were on the train two hours distant from Washington when Bunau-Varilla, knowingly disobeying their orders, affixed his signature They had ordered him to defer signing until they could review details, and they would have arrived in time had they not waited a day in New York to confer with Cromwell on his return from Paris. Cromwell reingratiated himself with Dr Amador, and later tried to get Bunau-Varilla removed

Bunau-Varilla's legacies to history are quite as confusing as Cromwell's. Each man, brilliant, audacious and vainglorious, would have the world believe that *he* was the father of the Republic of Panama.

Prolix and grandiose in his writing, Bunau-Varilla in his published books omitted significant facts which he related

## Coverups and Contradictions

in Paris in conversations with Don C. Seitz, business manager of *The World*, and William R. Hereford, its Paris correspondent. I worked intimately with these men and knew them as carefully trained, conscientious, truthful. What Bunau-Varilla told them on November 25 and 26, 1909, they had typed and verified and filed for possible future reference. What Bunau-Varilla told them will be resented as untrue by both Panamanian and North American friends who knew old Dr. Amador and his quiet ways. Here are quotations from "Statement of Philippe Bunau-Varilla" as Seitz and Hereford recorded them at the time:

When I (Bunau-Varilla) saw Amador in New York he came to my hotel and up to my rooms and announced that he intended to kill Cromwell because Cromwell had betrayed him and had led him into a revolution by false promises. Amador expected that his friends would be killed in Panama by Colombian troops and his and their property confiscated.

Cromwell, he (Amador) said, had been dodging him, had put him off and had finally failed him. I soothed Amador. Although he is an old usurer, he is a patriot, and undoubtedly would have killed Cromwell for having lied to him and promised things he could not fulfill. Cromwell was then in Paris in hiding. He had fled to Paris, in fear, to escape the vengeance of Amador.

Bunau-Varilla's furious hatred of Cromwell was more explicitly expressed in a book of some 30,000 words which he had his attorney, Frank D. Pavey of New York, present to the House Committee on Foreign Affairs, February 19, 1913. Pavey had been counsel to the Panamanian Legation in Washington while Bunau-Varilla was Panama's Minister.

The Bunau-Varilla book was accepted for the record of the hearings under the Rainey Resolution and was inserted as a preface, not as addenda, to "The Story of Panama" as printed in the 1913 edition of that Congressional document. It was not in the 1912 edition. The printed book, ostensibly written by Bunau-Varilla in Paris and signed by him March

29, 1912, was presented by Pavey with the representation that Bunau-Varilla had been detained and could not be present to testify and answer in person any questions the House Committee might wish to ask. But two days later Pavey wrote a letter of apology telling the Congressmen he hadn't been aware that Bunau-Varilla had already arrived in New York Bunau-Varilla was not called for questioning.

Most of Bunau-Varilla's 30,000 words were used up denouncing Cromwell and tearing to pieces Cromwell's bill of particulars supporting his demand for fees from the French canal company. He said Cromwell's statements were "entirely devoid of veracity". . "ridiculous" "perfidious" . . . . "odious" etc.!

In his conversation in Paris, as recorded at the time, Bunau-Varilla told how he, and he alone, made the arrangements in Washington for Dr. Amador and then provided the preliminary financing for the "revolution" His statement about President Theodore Roosevelt bears re-examination. In Paris Bunau-Varilla said:

"At the time of the revolution of Panama I did not know President Roosevelt, that is, I had met him only once just to shake hands with him, but afterward we got to know each other quite well."

On pages 310 and 311 of his 568-page book published in London in 1913, giving himself all the credit for creating the Republic of Panama, Bunau-Varilla disclosed that he was taken to the White House on October 9, 1903, by Assistant Secretary of State Francis B Loomis; that he had with President Roosevelt a friendly conversation about personal and political affairs, that T R asked him what he, Bunau-Varilla, thought would come out of the situation in Panama.

To this, Bunau-Varilla in his book, published ten years later, said he replied "in a slow, decided manner, Mr. President, a Revolution!"

T R's reactions in that conversation, according to Bunau-Varilla's book, led the French engineer to conclude that the

### Coverups and Contradictions 93

United States would not permit Colombia to put down a revolution in Panama, so he had Mme. Bunau-Varilla make a flag for the proposed republic, arranged all by himself the financing, and sent Dr Amador on his way.

The excerpt from the Seitz and Hereford memorandum reporting that Bunau-Varilla told them he had met T.R. "only once, just to shake hands with," becomes more interesting as one reads farther in their record of things Bunau-Varilla said to them in Paris. Bunau-Varilla talking:

He (T R.) once introduced me to a group of distinguished men as "the man to whom more than to any other we owe the Panama Canal." Someone mentioned Cromwell.

"Ho!" he laughed, and said loudly so that all could hear. "Cromwell! he's a faker!" I told Mr. Roosevelt when I left that there was one man who was a snake and who would do more harm than anyone else and that was Cromwell. "Well, I know," he (T.R.) said, "and I shall get rid of him."

Some historians have reported that T R. came to distrust Cromwell, but here was Bunau-Varilla's comment to Seitz and Hereford.

But he (T.R.) did not get rid of him, and afterward we find Cromwell on the same warship with Mr. Taft going to the Isthmus, and men have told me — men from Panama — "Cromwell must be all he claims to be for didn't he come on a government warship with Mr. Taft?" And we find Cromwell forcing Mr. Wallace, the engineer-in-chief, to deal with him. His influence is seen everywhere.

*The World* presented as much of "The Story of Panama" as could be told in 1912 to the Congressional Committee based in part upon Cromwell's bill of particulars supporting his claim for fees. It had assumed that Cromwell, as one of the most eminent lawyers of his day, was bound by a code of legal ethics and that he would not lie to prove the value of his legal and lobbying services. Now Bunau-Varilla was telling the Congressmen that "The Story of Panama" must be regarded as "equally devoid of veracity."

For example, he declared that the statement in "The Story of Panama" that he, Bunau-Varilla, had told Don Seitz in Paris that Cromwell had "made a contribution of $60,000 to the election fund of 1900" was "also a pure fiction." I prefer to believe what Seitz and Hereford wrote down at the time as Bunau-Varilla's statement to them. Here it is:

> Cromwell's fee was referred to a board of arbitration. He asked for $800,000 and got $200,000. He testified before that board that he had paid out of his own pocket $60,000 for "political purposes," saying that this was often done in America through the subscription to campaign funds. He said it wasn't bribery but perfectly proper and usual.

The French arbitrators who reduced Cromwell's fee and disbursements from $832,449.38 to $228,282.71 said the settlement offered by the French Panama Canal Company was "absolutely insufficient" and the amount demanded by Cromwell "exorbitant."

Paul Gontard, attorney for the New Panama Canal Company, told the aribtrators that Cromwell and his partners

> "affirm in support of their claim that they planned everything, directed everything, did everything, and obtained everything; that nothing was done without them, nor by anybody but themselves. Their affirmation is by no means exact."

Gontard further, said that Cromwell's claims for credit for inspiring the Spooner Bill, raising alarm over Nicaraguan volcanoes and initiating and directing Colombian diplomatic overtures were "gross exaggerations."

The arbitrators found that Cromwell's annual retainer of $10,000 had been paid by the French canal company regularly from October 1, 1889, to June 30, 1901 (when he was ordered to cease all activities), and that Cromwell had given his receipt in full "in behalf of himself and his law firm in payment of all accounts rendered up to June 30 1901, and in full discharge of all disbursements by me or my firm up to said date" — amounting to a total of $66,-443.78.

Further the arbitrators said: "Other efforts than theirs, no less enlightened and no less tenacious, contributed to the change in public opinion. In the history of the Isthmus and of the victory of Panama the name of Mr. Philippe Bunau-Varilla especially cannot be ignored."

Finally the court of Arbitration decreed on December 23, 1907, that since both parties had failed to prove their respective claims as to expenses each party should pay its own. And "in settlement of all accounts of every nature" the arbitrators awarded Cromwell and his firm for disbursements, $60,782.71 and for fees $167,500.

The arbitrators told Cromwell and his associates that the "fame of their success" in a matter of such world-wide importance as the Panama Canal would assure them of "an increase of reputation, an increase in their clientele," and "those who have linked their names to a great work, after having labored, are in great part rewarded by being honored."

Cromwell was made sole fiscal agent of the Republic of Panama in 1905 and resigned in 1937 because he was making Paris his residence for most of the time. He turned over the "Constitutional Fund" of $6,000,000, invested in more than 100 mortgages, to the Chase National Bank as fiscal agent. When he died in New York in 1948 at the age of 94, Cromwell left a gross estate of almost $19,000,000.

*Chapter 11*

# At Long Last T. R. Has "Nothing to Say!"

Facing in 1910 the showdown day in court, everyone in the Pulitzer organization who had dug into the Panama scandal was torn between resentment of the injustice of the Roosevelt charge of criminal libel and a sense of responsibility for the future of a free press.

If the Rooseveltian dictum prevailed, any editor could be dragged from his home and tried for libel in any distant federal jurisdiction where a copy of his paper had circulated. Pulitzer's *World* was rich, prosperous and powerful; it could stand the cost. But what if a little newspaper in Maine, for example, happened to have a subscriber, an army officer in the Presidio, and the editor published something that a politician in Washington said libeled him or the Government? The editor could be dragged to San Francisco, tried there in the Federal court — and ruined financially.

Theodore Roosevelt's determination to punish a critical press was too well known to be ignored In an unpublished dispatch Otto Carmichael, then chief of *The World's* Washington bureau, reported T.R.'s telling the Gridiron Club: "As to the men I am bringing libel suit against, I'll cinch them! I'll cinch them in the Federal courts if I can. If I can't cinch them there, I'll cinch them in the State courts. But one thing is sure: we'll cinch them!"

Those of us who knew in detail the masses of proof we had in hand to justify a defense on questions of fact, regretted the policy decision to attack the legality of the indictments *The World's* chief counsel, De Lancey Nicoll, believed we had enough facts to convince a jury, but the issue of freedom of the press, if abandoned to political chance, could vitally affect the future of America. "Who got the money?" could be answered later.

Joseph Pulitzer endorsed this view. "I think it is an act of public service," he wrote, "an act of special value to the entire press of the United States that these test questions should be adjudicated without any compromise whatsoever I am opposed not only to any compromise but to any delay or dilatory tactics."

So De Lancey Nicoll demurred to the indictment when *The World* as a corporation was brought to trial before Federal Judge Charles M. Hough in New York City, January 25, 1910 Argument paralleled that presented before Judge Albert B. Anderson, who had dismissed the parallel case against Delavan Smith and Charles R. Williams of the *Indianapolis News*, October 13, 1909. Judge Hough's decision, announced in the afternoon of January 26, 1910, as did the decision of Judge Anderson, held that there was no Federal libel law Judge Hough dismissed the jury, quashed the indictment, and suggested that the United States Supreme Court should be asked to interpret the statue for protection of harbor defenses before the Government attempted to use it to prosecute publishers.

By nightfall the brilliant mind of Mr. Pulitzer's editorial chief, Frank I Cobb, was at work on the Hough decision. His simple, precise, graphic writing had established Frank

Cobb as the most copied and respected editor of his generation. Don Seitz pressed him to save his energies and dictate to secretaries, but, long before the days of "do it yourself" Frank Cobb explained to me that he could better sense the value of his words if he typed his editorials himself on his own machine.

So *The World's* leading editorial of January 27, 1910, was a renewed challenge to Theodore Roosevelt. Newspapers of every shade of opinion responded favorably to the demand that the case be taken to the Supreme Court. Cobb's editorials hammered on that theme again and again, but a month passed before Washington assented to filing an appeal, on February 26, 1910. Argument on the appeal was not reached until October 24, 1910.

Cobb's first challenging editorial said:

"If there exists in Washington the shadow of a suspicion that a Federal libel law can be created by construction or interpretation — if there still remains the likelihood that some day another Roosevelt will prostitute his power by invoking the Act to Protect Harbor Defenses in order to prosecute newspapers that have offended him, and that every American newspaper is at the mercy of the President — then the sooner there is a final decision of the Supreme Court of the United States the better."

The Supreme Court's unanimous opinion finally affirming Judge Hough's quashing of the indictment was delivered January 3, 1911, by Chief Justice White Justice Harlan presided and Justices McKenna, Holmes, Day, Lurton and Hughes concurred

Frank Cobb's editorial the following morning said in part:

"There is no Federal libel law to muzzle American newspapers. Freedom of the press does not exist at the whim or pleasure of the President of the United States. It is at the mercy of no 'steward of the public welfare.' The rights and powers and authority of the States cannot be taken over by a usurping Federal Government...."

"While believing that the Panama articles printed in *The World* libelled nobody, we should have welcomed a trial of that issue on its merits had the case been brought in the State courts of New York by Mr. Roosevelt or any other person who considered himself aggrieved...

"The decision of the Supreme Court is so sweeping that no other President will be tempted to follow in the footsteps of Theodore Roosevelt, no matter how greedy he may be for power, no matter how resentful of opposition .... The great constitutional issue involved in the Roosevelt libel proceedings against *The World* is settled for all time. The freedom of the press is established beyond the power of Federal usurpation."

All the indictments against Joseph Pulitzer, Caleb M. Van Hamm and Robert Hunt Lyman of *The World* and Delavan Smith and Charles R Williams of the *Indianapolis News* were promptly dismissed.

Thus was won a victory for the freedom of the American press comparable in importance to the historic vindication of John Peter Zenger two centuries earlier.

Flashes of the Supreme Court finale came over the wires from Washington late in the afternoon. What would Theodore Roosevelt say?

T R was then Contributing Editor of the weekly *Outlook*. He had been the guest of honor at a reception in the Columbia Club in Indianapolis some time after Judge Anderson had thrown out the Roosevelt-ordered criminal indictment of the offending Indianapolis publishers. And it had been widely published that T.R. refused to shake hands with Judge Anderson in the receiving line and was quoted as having blurted out:

"A judge who would render such a decision as Anderson's in the Panama libel case is either a damned crook or a jackass!"

T.R. had started home from the *Outlook* office I hurried to Oyster Bay. It was cold waiting, that January 3, on the porch at Sagamore Hill, but *World* men didn't expect a warm welcome there.

At 7:20 P M. the Colonel arrived. Young son Quentin hurried down the steps to meet him To each of my questions T.R answered, "I have nothing to say."

Under the dimly lighted porte-cochere only the world-famous glistening teeth and eyeglasses of T.R. stood out in the reflection from the receding motorcar's lamps as I asked my final question.

"Colonel, won't you at least give the public the satisfaction of knowing whether your opinion of Judge Anderson now applies to the Supreme Court of the United States?"

His answer was as emphatic as his slamming of the great door at Sagamore Hill I had it set "all caps" in *The World* of January 4, 1911, and it has resounded in my memory ever since

"I HAVE NOTHING TO SAY!"

Seventy-nine days later, T R boasted before an audience of 8,000 at the University of California Charter Day celebration on the Berkeley campus, March 23, 1911·

"I took the Isthmus and left Congress to debate "

I could have asked T.R. at Sagamore Hill another question, but I had pledged Don Raoul Amador — a pledge released only by his death in Paris, March 23, 1934 — not to disclose the source of my information unless the Roosevelt libel suit against *The World* went to trial on questions of fact My question to T.R would have been:

"Did Dr. Manuel Amador and his son, Raoul, visit you in the White House, late at night, before Dr. Amador left for Panama to start the "revolution" and did you promise to see them through?"

*Chapter 12*

# *Dual Sovereignty Breeds Perpetual Discord*

If there is to be straight thinking by citizens of the United States and Panama on their rights, responsibilities and obligations in respect to the Panama Canal, an understanding of past and present relations is essential

All through the years of canal construction and intermittently ever since, administrative and defense problems have been fraught with annoyance and needless expense. The Taft Agreement of 1904 proved to be only a temporary adjustment of differences over tariff and commissary problems. Time and again United States authorities had to supervise Panamanian elections and supercede or supplant Panamanian police and, until 1955, supervise sanitation administrations

Radical and liberal elements in Panama were demanding as early as September, 1910, suppression of Article 136 of the Panamanian Constitution giving the United States the right to "reestablish public peace and constitutional order in the event of their being disturbed, provided the United

States shall, by public treaty, assume or have assumed the obligation of guaranteeing the independence and sovereignty of this Republic."

Opening of the Canal in 1914 increased Panamanian demands for reformation of the Hay-Bunau-Varilla Treaty of 1903. Discussion of bases for settling claims between Panama and the United States dragged on for years, until in October, 1933, a start was made toward implementing what President Franklin Delano Roosevelt called his "Good Neighbor Policy."

But the seeds of discord had been planted deep Statesmen who made the pattern at Panama seem not to have realized that friction is inevitable at any vital spot on earth where there is dual or overlapping sovereignty.

When earlier treaty negotiations were with the mother country, Colombia refused to include the cities of Panama and Colon in the proposed Canal Zone. Both lie entirely within the 10-mile-wide strip. Then, after T R. resorted to "taking" Panama, anything the United States proposed could have been obtained, but no one in authority had the foresight to include the terminal cities The "plan" of the Panama conspirators was to declare the independence of only the Canal Zone and the terminal cities, which were to be "brought under the protection of the United States" without reference to the rest of the Province

The need for a wide zone to include the entire watershed of the canal was recognized in a report to Congress by General Clarence E. Edwards, in command at Panama in 1916, but nothing was done.

Unofficially I had sounded the same warning of future needs in a signed article in *World's Work,* October, 1913, and again in an address before the Latin American Conference at Clark University, printed in *The Journal of Race Development,* Vol. 4, No. 4, April, 1914.

In this stand I had the advice of a close and trusted friend of my youth, the late Lindon W. Bates, internationally famous engineer. My *World's Work* article, reprinted also in

Spanish, was circulated widely in Latin America. In it I advocated:
1. Anticipating future needs, and taking then, as permitted by the Hay-Bunau-Varilla treaty of 1903 as "convenient and necessary," a Canal Zone 50 to 60 miles wide to include the entire watershed of the Canal.
2. Including the terminal cities of Panama and Colon to avoid the frictions that have existed ever since.
3. Inducing the Republic of Panama to establish its capital in the western highlands of the Province.
4. Returning the eastern end of the Province to Colombia as a gesture sentimentally more effective than the cash indemnity of $25,000,000 which the United States finally paid to Colombia in 1922.

I suggested that acquisition of territory for future defense could not be regarded as aggression — unless delayed until a new generation of Panamanians came to believe their "sovereignty" an inalienable right. They believe it now. For Panama history books have not told Panamanian youth that only a handful of conspirators knew that a "revolution" was planned.

Radical ideologies infiltrated all around the Canal Zone and exaggerated ideas of super-nationalism took hold of a generation of Panamanians schooled to believe in the fiction that their "founding fathers" actually *won* their independence.

So uninformed and misinformed Panamanians and North Americans took for granted the rightousness of Franklin Delano Roosevelt's abrogation of practically everything in the 1903 treaty to which the Panamanian politicians objected. The new treaty, signed in Washington, March 2, 1936, by Ricardo J. Alfaro and Narciso Garay for Panama and by Secretary of State Cordell Hull and Assistant Secretary Sumner Welles for the United States, was not ratified by the United States Senate because of opposition, until July 25, 1939. This treaty gave the Republic of Panama an entirely new status.

Those now responsible for public and governmental attitudes in Panama were not born, or were children at the time of the "revolution." They were adults when their Alfaro-Hull Treaty of 1936 was ratified in 1939. But little did they realize the momentous import of that first step. For it was the beginning of Uncle Sam's world-wide giveaways.

The giveaway series did not start, as so many have supposed, with the Marshall Plan in 1947, nor at Yalta in 1945, nor at Teheran in 1943. The giveaways started when F.D.R. pitched into the Panamanian politicians' hands the priceless treaty rights of the United States to build defense bases outside the ten-mile-wide Canal Zone.

That giveaway cost American taxpayers much more than the million-dollars in rental paid to the Panama Government during World War II for permission to plant guns, build roads, landing fields, bomber bases and nearly 400 buildings on Panama's pasture lands and in her swamps and jungles adjacent to the Canal Zone.

It took endless negotiation to obtain **permission** — where the United States formerly had the **right** under the 1903 treaty — to use Panamanian territory for defense purposes. Finally the United States Army was forced by action of the Panama National Assembly to withdraw in 1948 and abandon buildings and improvements which had cost well over another million dollars to create

Article I of the 1903 treaty was eliminated. It read "The United States guarantees and will maintain the independence of the Republic of Panama."

The 1903 treaty granted to the United States "in **perpetuity** the use, occupation and control" not only of the Canal Zone but also of "**any other lands and waters outside of the Zone which may be necessary and convenient for the construction, maintenance, operation, sanitation and protection of the said enterprise.**"

And, further, under the 1903 treaty, Panama granted to the United States

"all the rights, power and authority within the zone . . . .

and within the limits of all auxiliary lands and waters . which the United States would possess **if it were the sovereign** of the territory within which said lands and waters are located, to the **exclusion of the exercise by the Republic of Panama of any such sovereign rights, power or authority."**

All United States authority outside the Canal Zone was abrogated in the following clause of the 1936-39 treaty:

"The United States of America hereby *renounces* the grant made to it in perpetuity by the Republic of Panama of the use, occupation and control of lands and waters, in addition to those now under the jurisdiction of the United States of America outside the zone.... which may be necessary and convenient for the construction, maintenance, operation, sanitation and protection of the Panama Canal or of any auxiliary canals or other works necessary and convenient for the construction, maintenance, operation, sanitation and protection of the said enterprise."

Then, having abandoned its rights to defense bases outside the Canal Zone, the United States agreed with Panama, in Article II of the 1936-39 treaty, that "if, in the event of some now unforeseen contingency" land outside the Canal Zone should be needed, the two governments

"will agree upon such measures as it may be necessary to take in order to insure the maintenance, sanitation, efficient operation and effective protection of the Canal, in which the two countries are jointly and vitally interested."

The United States Government's right of eminent domain in acquiring property within the cities of Panama and Colon which might be needed for canal operation was renounced.

Also eliminated was the right of the United States to maintain public order in Panama if the Panamanian Government could not do so.

And the annuity of $250,000 paid by the United States for use of the canal strip was increased to $430,000 —on account of the Roosevelt devaluation of the dollar.

The 1936-39 treaty made many other concessions to Panama. It restricted residence in the Canal Zone to American civilian and military personnel, established "corridors" within the Zone for Panamanian convenience, and prohibited new private enterprises in the Canal Zone.

The effect of the treaty ratification in July, 1939, was summarized in such headlines as. "The U.S in Panama Pact Quits as Guardian Becomes Neighbor — New Treaty Ends the Right of Intervention, Substituting Bilateral Cooperation."

Acquisition of bases for defense of the Canal became imperative when war in Europe started in September, 1939. Thereupon administrative annoyances multiplied. Communist infiltration as well as Nazi influences in Panama came to the surface.

Labor union organizers flocked in from Mexico and from the United States Most of the Panamanian employees on the Canal had been unionized by the CIO. Many of them are children of West Indian laborers who were imported to help build the Canal and who have become Panamanian citizens Most of the skilled employees, citizens of the United States, were unionized by the AFL.

Red unionism, under the Latin American leadership of Vicente Lombardo Toledano of Mexico, has had its toehold in Panama since Lombardo and the late Philip Murray of the CIO were photographed together for their joint promotion pamphlet "Labor's Good Neighbor Policy."

United States Army and Navy and Canal authorities were necessarily tight-lipped about the annoyances attending their use of more than 130 defense sites. Obtaining access wasn't always painless, but responsible Panama officials were generally cooperative. The big question was *"How much?"*

A defense sites agreement was not finally signed in Panama until May 18, 1942. Vivid memories of the situation in Panama preceding the Pearl Harbor crisis came to us during a brief visit there in September, 1941. Major General Daniel Van Voorhis, commander of the area, was leaving for New York, and he invited Mrs. Harding and me to be his guests on the bridge of the ship to witness the salute of many U S. airplanes circling Colon Harbor. Waving toward the west bank, the General told us: "Those jungles are bristling with guns."

Beneficent as those guns seemed to Panama, with World War II threatening to spread, the Defense Sites Agreement, signed after General Van Voorhis' retirement, granted to the United States only "temporary use for defense purposes of the lands referred to in the attached Memorandum." Details of that Memorandum were kept secret, but it was already known that the United States was building at Rio Hato, on Panamanian territory west of the Canal Zone, what was then the largest air base in the world. Also it was well understood that several bases of great strategic value were included in the then unmentionable total of more than 130 defense sites.

The Agreement stipulated that "The Republic of Panama retains its sovereignty over the areas" and that all buildings "shall become the property of the Republic of Panama upon the termination of their use by the United States." The bases were to be evacuated one year after ratification of a definitive treaty of peace — not just after a cease-fire.

Some of the defense sites were small areas for observation towers, searchlight or gun emplacements. Others were outlying uninhabited islands, some were broad pastures or cleared jungle made into landing fields The total amounted to many thousands of acres.

Most of the land and water had little monetary value except in the minds of some Panamanian politicians who emphasized its "international importance" and suggested rental as high as $1,600 per acre per year!

But neither protection of the Canal and their own country nor the gravy flowing into their treasury silenced the anti-American elements. Clamor against "yanqui aggression" was popular even during the war, and was intensified immediately after V-J Day by anti-American clamor to get United States forces out of Panamanian territory.

Spruille Braden, Assistant Secretary of State for Latin America, was keeping himself informed of every move in Panama. His judgments were based on his early experience in engineering and business in Latin America, his success in negotiating the Chaco Peace that ended the bloody war between Bolivia and Paraguay, his ambassadorships in Argentina, Colombia and Cuba He knew, as few do, the essential elements of Latin American bargaining.

So Secretary Braden called the Pentagon and inquired whether it would be possible, for bargaining purposes, to authorize the State Department to say, through diplomatic channels, that the United States was willing to relinquish 20, or perhaps 30 of the less important defense sites and keep the rest. Mr. Braden knew the strategic value of the big Rio Hato base, and he knew also that the best-intentioned men in the Panamanian Government would have to resist radical and communist pressures. We would still hold a hundred defense sites over which to bargain.

But the Pentagon, lacking his experience and vision, told Secretary Braden that it wanted to keep *all* the sites. Then, without consultation or advice, without giving State Department either time or opportunity to drive a bargain, Pentagon announced in Washington on September 2, 1946, that it was handing back to Panama 65 defense sites covering more than 10,000 acres, and that defense sites rentals of $975,587 had been paid up to June 10, 1945.

This Pentagon announcement of September 2, 1946 came on the same day that the Panama Assembly voted unanimously to *demand* that the United States evacuate all defense sites immediately And on the following day, Panama's President Enrique Jimenez announced that occupation of future defense sites would not even be discussed until all had been returned!

Thereupon United States Ambassador Frank T. Hines left

for Washington, and on September 12, 1946, a joint statement of the two governments announced that defense sites problems would be resolved by "friendly negotiations." A firmer stand, earlier, might well have averted the later compromise whereby the future of the Rio Hato base is left, after fifteen years, to still more political haggling under our giveaway treaty of 1955.

The Pentagon retreat of 1946 left the door wide open for more agitation. President Jimenez was quoted as demanding that the United States revise its whole attitude toward his country and make the 1936-39 treaty — the F.D.R. giveaway — more effective in terms of *benefits* for Panama."

The hope of the Administration in Washington was that Jose Antonio Remon, who succeeded Jimenez as President of Panama, would be able to stay in office throughout his four-year term, which began October 1, 1952.

Whether the voice of Moscow, resounding in the UN, could stir up more discord in Panama was still a point to be watched In November, 1946, the Soviet made a furious attack in the UN on the United States, charging that its defense bases around the world are evidence of "aggression."

Alger Hiss, who was active in drafting the UN Charter at San Francisco, was then head of the Office of Political Affairs of the State Department Without consulting or advising Spruille Braden, Assistant Secretary of State for Latin America, Hiss sent to the UN a list of America's "occupied territories," and included in that list the Panama Canal Zone

That gave Panama a text Ricardo J. Alfaro, then Panama's Foreign Minister and Chairman of its UN delegation, in a speech before the Trusteeship Committee of the UN, declared that Panama **retains its sovereignty over the Canal Zone** and that the State Department's report should be corrected.

Newspaper headlines gave the Assistant Secretary of State for Latin America his first inkling that such a report had been issued. Hiss could not be found that day to recall it. Secretary Braden demanded a showdown, because he was responsible for negotiations in behalf of our military authorities, who insisted that we still needed the bases in Panama. The Hiss report strengthened opposition of the Panamanian politicians while Braden was assuring the Pentagon of State Department support to get the bases under the terms of the 1936-39 treaty.

But Dean Acheson, then Acting Secretary of State, backed up Hiss.

"I was infuriated by the stupidity — which I then thought it was — of putting the Panama Canal Zone in the category of occupied territories," Secretary Braden told me, "but I did not realize its full significance as a play into Russian hands until after Hiss' other activities were exposed."

Mr. Braden later recalled that immediately following the "assist by Hiss" a dispatch from London reported Parliament's being told by its very-left Labor member, **Zilliacus, that the United States should turn over control of the Panama Canal to the UN and that Britain should do likewise with Gibraltar and Suez.**

On December 9, 1947, Dr. Alfaro resigned as Foreign Minister in protest against his government's agreeing to consider extending the leases on thirteen bases, the most important ones, which were then occupied by the United States.

Following Alfaro's lead, the Panama Assembly on December 23, 1947, unanimously rejected lease extension. Anti-American mobs surrounded the legislature vowing to lynch any member voting for the leases, and students and teachers threatened to call a general strike.

So the United States, in January, 1948, abandoned the thirteen defense sites and retreated within its Canal Zone. It was then understood that future defense would be entirely from within the Zone limits

Diplomatic retreat by the United States led only to more demands In October, 1952, eight ex-presidents, six former

## Dual Sovereignty Breeds Perpetual Discord 111

ministers of foreign relations of Panama and spokesmen for Panama labor unions and the Panama Chamber of Commerce were witnesses before a foreign relations committee of the Panama National Assembly. On November 17, 1952, the National Assembly voted unanimously to demand another general revision of treaty relations with the United States

This chapter of the untold story is condensed from the first of a series written by me as a Vice President of the National Economic Council, Inc., of New York, and published in 1953-54-55-56. The late Representative Lawrence H. Smith, Republican of Wisconsin, made this reference to them in addressing the House on January 17, 1957.

"Following the crisis of Suez, precipitated on July 26, 1956, world attention increasingly focused on the Panama Canal and United States policies concerning its control and operation, with persistent demands for some form of internationalization for that American waterway.

"The writings of recent years on the Panama Canal are numerous, with many articles reprinted in the *Congressional Record*. Notable among them was a series by Earl Harding, distinguished journalist, business executive, and lifelong student of Latin American relations, including the history of the Panama Canal. Mr Harding's first article in the series was published September 1, 1953, entitled 'It Started at Panama.'

"In the light of subsequent events, this paper was prophetic Not only that, it supplies extremely pertinent information on the start of our foreign-aid programs, which should be read by all Members of Congress and other leaders of the Nation.

"To make the indicated paper in Mr. Harding's series readily available in the annals of the Congress along with the last three, which have already been reprinted in the Appendix of the Congressional Record, I include its text."

My prediction on September 1, 1953, was: "If Panama's

desire for still further concessions is not satisfied, pressure in behalf of Panama such as Alger Hiss in 1946 brought to bear through the United Nations may take the form of demanding internationalization of the Panama Canal "

In response to agitation described by some Panamanians as "a demand for a showdown with the United States," President Remon appointed as a special negotiating committee. Roberto M. Heurtematte, Panama's Ambassador to Washington; Dr Octavio Fabrega, former Minister of Foreign Relations, and Carlos Sucre, former Minister of Government. They were to start their work in Washington by September 10, 1953.

*Chapter 13*

# 1955 Giveaway Treaty Jammed Through—
# "Mutual Consent" Is Only Way Out

Diplomatic conversations over Panama's demands for further treaty revision continued in Washington from September 10, 1953, until the end of 1954. But, for the most part, details were "top secret" at both ends, even after President Jose Antonio Remon and his attractive Senora, with an entourage of ten, arrived in Washington in late September, 1953, and remained for a fortnight. Remon told 300 guests of the Pan American Society in New York, October 2, 1953 "I didn't come to this country to ask for money, I came to ask for justice, and by justice I mean Panama should receive its proper share of the great enterprise that is the Canal."

To accelerate its diplomatic drive, the Remon Administration retained two retired United States Army public relations experts, Generals Julius Klein and Kenneth Buchanan of Chicago The "nature and purpose" of their employment, as recorded in the Foreign Agents Registration Section of the Department of Justice in Washington, was to

serve the government of Panama "as public relations counsel with regard to its (Panama's) efforts and aims to bring about a satisfactory adjustment of its relations with the U.S.A by way of treaty amendment and other forms of aid."

Total recorded fees and expenses of these experts from the date of their engagement up to the termination of their employment, December 31, 1953, amounted to $20,245.22.

The Remons' visits in Washington and New York created favorable impressions By midsummer of 1954 the fact that the United States had been kicked off its defense bases in Panama had faded into the background of publicity over Panama's being blessed for the first time in many years with what appeared to be a stable government.

The treaty negotiators, trying hard to earn their $50 daily allowances, did their best to prove that a profitable, cooperative partnership between the United States and the Republic of Panama was now possible They pointed to many acts of genuine friendship under the Remon regime. His Congress had outlawed Communism. He had fired notorious Red teachers Apparently good use was being made of big loans and of more than a million dollars a year of United States "technical cooperation" funds applied, with many American technicians, to Panamanian agriculture, education, housing, public health and social welfare. They needed 100 more social workers!

Most pressing, at that time, was Panama's desire to increase the United States annuity for use of the Canal Zone from $430,000 to a minimum of $5,000,000 or to 20 per cent of gross canal tolls, then around $37,500,000 a year. Panamanian radicals didn't begin until later demanding "at least 50/50 division"

My comment then, in a National Economic Council Letter which Senator Thomas E Martin placed in the *Congressional Record,* August 20, 1954, seems, in retrospect, to explain a perpetual thought in the little Republic:

> Don't blame Panama's statesmen. Theirs is only the UN-iversal urge — "Get all you can from Uncle Sam!" In

order to hold their political jobs they must tell the populace that their little country is entitled to a "fair share" in what they represent to be an "enormously profitable" canal enterprise. Gross tolls are the talking point, not the small net.

By midsummer of 1954 the treaty negotiators' delays were causing Panamanian patience to wear thin. Typical of the intermittent meddling from partisans in Panama was a letter in *Newsweek*, signed by a Panamanian, warning the United States:

Pressure is building up in Panama among the masses . . Many are asking themselves how long will President Remon be able to continue without explaining to the public why negotiations should be delayed so long . . . . Imagine the repercussions should Panama decide after, say, one year of ineffectual negotiation, to recall their mission.

President Remon was quoted as saying he would not retreat one step from his demand for "justice" from the United States But a Panamanian assassin's bullet, January 2, 1955, did not permit him to witness his triumph. And, up to this writing, his assassins have not been punished. The treaty, which gave Panama almost everything Remon had demanded. was signed in Washington, January 25, 1955, ratified by Panama March 15, 1955 and sent to the United States Senate on May 9, 1955.

State Department negotiators rejected the Panamanians' demand to terminate at the end of 99 years United States rights in the Canal Zone, granted *in perpetuity* by the 1903 treaty. Panama's disappointment was voiced in an 8-column headline across the front page of the Panama *Star & Herald*, February 3, 1955: "U.S. Rejected Time Limit on C.Z Concession."

But in the United States, secrecy which shrouded these vital negotiations for sixteen months was scarcely penetrated by the North American press, either during the deliberations of the Senate Committee on Foreign Relations or after ratification of the giveaway, July 29, 1955.

The Senate's inadequate consideration of the long, involved giveaway treaty and its "Memorandum of Understandings" occupied only a fraction of the one day, July 29, 1955, when ratification was rushed through. The Rhodes scholar Senator Fulbright of Arkansas, in his leading argument for ratification, assured the Senate that the treaty "establishes the framework for the basic relationship between the United States and the Republic of Panama" and that "the treaty does not affect our present rights and relations in any respect whatsoever."

Senator Russell of Georgia repeatedly questioned the wisdom of ratification. Otherwise what passed for "debate" failed to show up the seriousness of commitments made by the State Department negotiators.

As Panamanian demands pile up in the future — as they have continually ever since ratification — this brief quotation from Senator Russell's argument against ratification will be worth remembering:

I reiterate that the Department of Defense never thinks of challenging the Department of State or interfering in any way in any international negotiations. That has been true of all negotiations we have had in the past two years.

If I had the privilege of appointing someone in the Department of Defense I would have cautioned him, when he came to consider a treaty having to do with the Panama Canal, to get some agreement *that would not bleed us white*, if we had to get some land outside the zone, in the event of another war . . . . while we were committing ourselves to these increased payments, we should have some room to stand and fight, in the event of another war, rather than having to pay a large rental for additional ground.

Ratification was voted, 72 to 14. Senators voting to reject the giveaway treaty were Byrd, Case of South Dakota, Ervin, Gore, Jackson, Johnston of South Carolina, Kerr, Long, Magnuson, Neuberger, Robertson, Russell, Stennis and Thurmond.

## 1955 Giveaway Treaty Jammed Through

The most conspicuous concessions to Panama, thus ratified by the United States Senate, were:

1. Increased the United States annuity to Panama from $430,000 (originally $250,000 before gold dollar devaluation) to $1,930,000 This must mean either increased tolls, burdening all shipping, or increased drain on American taxpayers. American ship owners were already protesting that tolls were too high, and were preparing their suit to compel a reduction. (They lost their appeal to the U S. Supreme Court, April 28, 1958.)
2. Gave Panama, without compensation, waterfront and other properties, including Panama Railroad's yards and terminals in the cities of Colon and Panama, of an "estimated fair market value," as stated by our government of $24,300,000. These gifts included the Hotel Washington in Colon, worth $1,450,000, Colon Hospital, market value $1,400,000, and many other parcels
3. Agreed to ask Congress to appropriate and authorize building a bridge across the Panama Canal to replace the Thatcher Ferry, estimated to cost up to $27,000,000.

The proposed giving away of the Panama Railroad properties fitted into plans of the then top management of the Panama Canal to abandon the railroad and replace it with a new truck highway Congress decided that the Panama Railroad should be kept, but permitted the Canal management to give to Panama the railroad terminals in Panama and Colon.

Other concessions to Panama were designed to restrict American and extend Panamanian rights in respect to commissary privileges, trade advantages, wage differentials, taxation, etc

Panama's principal token return for all the treaty concessions was "the right to use, for a period of fifteen years without cost," as a military training and maneuver base the old

Rio Hato base west of the Canal Zone. Extension after 15 years is subject to "agreement between the two governments."

But Panamanian law and sovereignty over the Rio Hato area was not affected American soldiers, ordered to drill there, lost the protection of their own country, just as United States forces in other parts of the world lost their rights under the Status of Forces Treaty.

Deep-rooted problems affecting the entire future of the Panama Canal are tied into the strait-jacket of the "Treaty of 1955" — which may be modified, as its predecessor treaties between the United States and the Republic of Panama have been modified, *only by "mutual consent."*

*Chapter 14*

# Just Who Are Backing the Drives to Internationalize, and to Nationalize

Nasser's July 26, 1956, seizure of the Suez Canal and, six months later, his "Egyptianization by seizure" of all British and French financial institutions in his country, shocked an unsuspecting and unprepared world

Equally unsuspecting and unprepared for a continuing crisis in their own area were those North Americans whose eyes have been on Europe, on NATO, on the Far East and the Middle East, while their usual sources of intelligence failed to alert them to the extent of the propaganda for *internationalization* — even for *nationalization by Panama* — of the Panama Canal. On the heels of the Suez crisis Panama began anew to proclaim that it has sovereign rights over the Canal Zone and will never surrender them.

The agitation for internationalizing or for "Panamanianizing" the Panama Canal has been astonishingly better known in Latin America than in the United States. North Americans have taken too long for granted that the canal is working well, that it is safe as a lifeline of national defense, and that United States relations with Latin American neighbors have been steadily improving President Eisenhower's presence at the InterAmerican Conference of Chief Executives at Panama in July, 1956, followed immediately by Secretary of State John Foster Dulles' goodwill mission farther south, was interpreted as signifying that Franklin Delano Roosevelt's "Good Neighbor Policy" was being surely revitalized

The cap sheaf, so far as North American readers and listeners knew, was President Eisenhower's recommendation at Panama that the twenty-one American Republics should coordinate their planning through one central committee to report to the Organization of American States. Such a committee met in Washington and, on September 19, 1956, under the chairmanship of the President's brother, Dr. Milton Eisenhower, drew up a list of problems, for future consideration, requiring technical assistance and economic aid As the reader may guess, all of that aid would come out of the pockets of United States taxpayers

It may have been only by coincidence that Luis Quintanilla, Mexican career diplomat, was noticeably active behind the scenes of the Panama Conference of 1956. He was minister, then ambassador, to Moscow, 1942-45 — a period when the coloration of the Mexican government attracted foreign attention I was told by highly informed authority that Quintanilla's friendship for the Soviet Hierarchy was so pronounced that it set badly with anti-Communist members of the Organization of American States and impeded his advancement in that body.

It happened — or did it just *happen*? — that the Conference of Chief Executives of the Western Hemisphere was projected for the very week when Nasser was to seize the Suez Canal. If Nasser had "planned it that way" he could not have plotted a more effective diversion of attention from his own objective The Moscow-directed center in Prague for training Communist spies and infiltration experts was then busy preparing for more deviltry in Latin America.

The Prague activity was disclosed to American readers in a dispatch from Bonn, Germany, released by the *North American Newspaper Alliance* under the by-line of Omer Anderson.

This dispatch from Bonn was headlined in Washington, in *The Evening Star* of September 13, 1956: "RED PLOT AGAINST U.S ON PANAMA CANAL." It detailed Red plans to spread anti-United States propaganda lies throughout Latin America and to use the Panama Canal as its most effective hate vehicle

And, eight months later, the alert *Evening Star* front-paged the news on May 3, 1957, that Moscow radio, broadcasting in Spanish, warned Mexico and Central America that American military maneuvers around the Panama Canal in April of 1957 were "intended to frighten the people of Panama, who insist on return of territories occupied by the United States"

Agitation for internationalization of the Panama Canal is not a new, although a little known, story As far back as 1946 Red lanterns lighted its beginning The Suez crisis, after a lapse of ten years, threw new light on that spectrum.

Twenty days after the Suez seizure, Ralph E Flanders, then a Republican United States Senator of Vermont, stated publicly in Victoria, B.C., on August 15, 1956, that internationalization of the Panama Canal could ease the Egyptian crisis

Again on September 9, at Swarthmore, Pennsylvania, addressing the Society for Social Responsibility in Science, Senator Flanders as reported in *The New York Times* of September 10, 1956, said internationalization of the Panama Canal would give Nasser a "face-saving precedent" for agreeing to internationalization of Suez.

Also James P Warburg, ex-banker, prolific author and son of the late Paul M. Warburg, in a 400-word letter in *The New York Times* of September 12, 1956, urged that the Panama Canal be placed "under international or United

Nations control" as "a bridge over which President Nasser could, without losing face, retreat from his present refusal to accept a similar control over the Suez waterway."

Warburg renewed his campaign in a column-long letter in *The New York Times* of January 5, 1957, and later in speeches, in a conspicuously promoted radio interview, and in a signed article in a left-wing magazine called *The Reporter* Senator Hubert M. Humphrey, Democrat of Minnesota, introduced the magazine article in the *Congressional Record* of March 25, 1957, and a long Warburg speech expanding the same theme. The United Press spread the Warburg letter of January 5, 1957, into Latin American newspapers. So did propaganda multiply.

For the sake of historical accuracy I asked Senator Flanders whether he or Warburg was the father of the idea, since it appeared almost simultaneously. The Senator replied that he "made the first suggestion in Victoria, B.C. on August 15" and that he was "quite unfamiliar at the time with any position that Mr. Warburg had taken."

But the Vermont Senator did not lead the publicity parade One week ahead of him, on August 9, 1956, former President Harry S. Truman recommended to the Democratic National Convention in Chicago that the Suez and Panama canals be placed in the jurisdiction of the United Nations This drew a front-page headline in *The Washington Post* of August 10: "TRUMAN URGES CONTROL OF VITAL CANALS BY UN"

The Chicago dispatch said Truman "told the Democratic Platform Committee that when he was at the Potsdam Conference in 1945 he had suggested and argued without success for two days in favor of making international waterways out of the Panama Canal, the Suez Canal, the Black Sea Straits, the Rhine-Danube Canal and the Kiel Canal."

Secretary of State Dulles countered the Truman publicity by a press conference assertion that a search of State Department records of the Potsdam Conference showed no such statement by Truman. Still Drew Pearson in his syndicated column published in Washington on January 4, 1957, said Truman had told him in an interview as early as February 19, 1956, that he, Truman, would have put both Suez and Panama under the United Nations.

And Truman in a copyrighted signed article released by the *North American Newspaper Alliance* and published widely on January 13, 1957, reiterated in substance his earlier assertion. He said that at Potsdam he urged that all the canals be made "free waterways for merchant shipping."

Another case of "internationalitis" broke out on the January 20, 1957, editorial page of *The Washington Post*, Eugene Meyer's richly financed daily, the only morning newspaper in the nation's capital. "LET UN GUARANTEE ALL BIG WATERWAYS" was the head over Herbert Elliston's "Second Look" — the title he used on his column as contributing editor.

Born in England in 1895, Herbert Berridge Elliston started his widely varied career on small English dailies. He came to the United States in 1921. As listed in *Who's Who*, he was economic advisor to the Chinese Government, 1923-27, research economist of the Council on Foreign Relations, New York, 1927-30, financial editor and columnist of *The Christian Science Monitor*, Boston, 1930-40, and since 1940 either editor or contributing editor of *The Washington Post*.

(The *Who's Who* listing was inaccurate Young Elliston was only the assistant to the adivsor, not of the Chinese Government but of Chang Tso-lin, pro-Communist war lord of Manchuria. A sympathetic attitude toward Chinese Communists carried over noticeably into some of Elliston's editorial pages in Washington.)

Elliston argued that "the time is now ripe to revive the Potsdam 1945 idea for .. all major international waterways .... and a supervision of tolls undertaken by the United. Nations .... How would this affect the Panama Canal Zone? The juridical sovereign is the Republic of Panama, but the United States retains control of the zone in a partnership agreement with Panama signed in 1936. There need be no change in the arrangement."

Late, by seven months, in joining the 1956 claque for "internationalizing" the Panama Canal was Congressman James Roosevelt, of Los Angeles, son of the President who started in 1936 giving away United States treaty rights in Panama Press association dispatches from Chicago, March 25, 1957, quoted Roosevelt as telling a bond drive that the United States should turn over its Canal to the United Nations provided Nasser will throw in Suez, and that "we can't expect one nation to agree to give up its sovereign power unless we are willing to do the same thing."

*The Americas Daily*, published in Miami Springs, Florida, and widely distributed by airmail, in bold front-page headlines spread the James Roosevelt proposal across Latin America

This internationalization propaganda inched steadily ahead in 1956 and 1957, although it received slight attention from North Americans But Britain's Labor Party leaders, Clement Atlee and Hugh Gaitskell, year-end visiting lecturers in the United States, contributed to university students in Ann Arbor and Cambridge their advice that Uncle Sam should give his Panama Canal to the United Nations.

This same line of propaganda for internationalizing the Panama Canal was reiterated by Truman and Clement Atlee in a filmed TV interview by Edward R. Murrow over the Columbia Broadcasting System on November 30, 1958.

⁂

Historians may in time run to earth the paternity of this giveaway idea For now, let us see how Dictator Nasser's example of canal expropriation inspired Panamanian youth — those who will be the Panamanian politicians with whom Uncle Sam will have to reckon in the future. In their kindly tropical atmosphere both "giveaway" and "getmore" flourish.

"*Panamanian Students Declare Their Position Regarding Canal Problems*" was the bold headline on page one of the

*September 7, 1956 issue of The Americas Daily.* A 250-word dispatch, dated Panama, gave details of "declarations approved by the University Students General Assembly."

Their first demand was for the Government of Panama to denounce the Hay-Bunau-Varilla Treaty of 1903 "as against international law and the most elementary principles of equity and justice."

(Panamanian youth might well have been reminded that wiping out the original treaty might leave their country in its former status as a province or department of Colombia.)

Next in significance, the Student Assembly resolved "to recognize that Egypt, in nationalizing the Suez Canal, acted in legitimate exercise of its sovereign rights."

Looking to the future, the Student Assembly called for creation of a National Assembly of prominent citizens to formulate national thinking on international problems, and for the appointment of a commission of university professors and students to "study and consider the different aspects of a possible nationalization or internationalization of the Panama Canal."

In a final burst of patriotic enthusiasm the Student Assembly resolved —

"to declare that we Panamanians express our invariable determination to nationalize the Panama Canal as a permanent aspiration"

The seeds of Panamanian discontent, scattered to the winds by the Student Assembly, sprouted in March, 1957, in an International Conference on Interoceanic Canals sponsored by the University of Panama. Intellectuals were present from Mexico, the Central American countries and Cuba, but representatives of the United States were not mentioned in press reports of the round table sessions.

Some conflicting opinions were expressed, but the *United Press* reported "an agreement in certain degree about Panama's right to revision of her treaties with the United

States." Cesar Quintero, of Panama, was among those demanding abrogation of rights "in perpetuity" in the Canal Zone granted to the United States in the Hay-Bunau-Varilla Treaty of 1903 Former Foreign Minister Octavio Fabrega, who led Panama's negotiators in wangling the 1955 giveaway treaty out of the State Department, said the "perpetuity" grant should be considered invalid because inconsistent with Panamanian sovereignty

Fabio Fournier, of the University of Costa Rica, was quoted as predicting the creation, possibly by the United Nations, of an international juridic mechanism to prescribe rules for the operation of interoceanic canals.

Although there were no official decisions by this international conference, according to *United Press* reports "the Latin American jurists had, in general, the opinion that Panama should get bigger compensation from the Canal " Vicente Saenz, of Mexico, was quoted as stating that Panama has the right to claim 50 per cent of the Panama Canal's revenues after the United States recovers its capital investment.

The United States' net investment of $489,162,524 and what the Canal has done for Panama get slight mention when a Red-inspired mob shouts "down with the Yanquis!"

This line of propaganda in the University of Panama's March, 1957, International Conference on Interoceanic Canals was echoed in a letter to the *Times* of London by Panama's Ambassador to Britain, Roberto Arias, as quoted by the *United Press* on May 1, 1957· "Panama has never received for the use of its geographic resources a compensation that can be described as just or equitable."

Confirmation of the extent of such propaganda came to me in May, 1957, from an American businessman just returned from one of his regular visits to his company's extensive properties in Brazil and Argentina. Also, on April 17, 1957, Representative Daniel J. Flood of Pennsylvania told Congress:

".... recently returning travelers from Latin American countries report wide-spread agitation to get the United States, including its armed forces, out of the Panama area, with the ultimate aim of turning jurisdiction over the Canal enterprise to Panama or the United Nations

"The pattern of this program is obvious It conforms to the well-known and long-standing communistic plan to place the United States on the defensive by using the Panama Canal as a psychological lever to cause anti-American feeling as well as to wrest from the United States its authority and control over the Canal."

° ° °

How far, how fast, and in what unexpected directions will the Panama Canal "nationalization" and "internationalization" propaganda spread? How serious is it? How dangerous? It is not too late, now, to measure the impact of such propaganda at home as well as abroad.

*The Methodist Reporter,* an unofficial church organ described by its publishers in Nashville, Tennessee, as "A private news service for the professional leadership of The Methodist Church," printed in its issue of December 4, 1956, the following editorial

"*America's Secret Weapon*

"The United States has a secret weapon greater than the H-bomb, but completely harmless to life and limb. If thrown into the touchy Suez situation at this time, it would have a greater effect than all the invading nations or the UN has had

"Our secret weapon is the Panama Canal Christian leaders at work in International affairs have proposed for years that the Suez Canal, the Panama Canal, the Straits of Gibraltar, and the Straits of Singapore be put under international control. Principle behind this suggestion is that these waterways are so vital to so many nations that no one nation should have control over them.

"The United States has already placed itself in the role of peacemaker in the Suez fracas. It can now show its complete sincerity and desire for peace by offering to the

United Nations complete control over the Panama Canal. Such an offer would indeed be a bombshell in the midst of Suez crisis But this is not a give-away.

"This offer should be made only on these conditions

"(1) The Suez Canal would also be turned over to the complete control of the United Nations.

"(2) That Panama and Egypt receive the same amount of money they have been receiving, as rental for operation of the canals within their respective borders

"(3) That profits from operations of the canals be used for the budget of the United Nations.

"(4) In the event the United Nations ever becomes extinct or inactive, ownership of the Panama Canal would revert to the United States

"Details can be worked out by the nations involved The United States, as a very influential member of the U.N., would still have a large hand in the operation of the Panama Canal, Britain and France, in the same way, would still be active in running the Suez Canal

"Made in the spirit of peace on earth, good will toward all men, such a gift to the 79 nations in the UN should certainly please the Prince of Peace at this Christmastide Is it too much to ask of a Christian nation?

"We believe that Methodists, joining hands with other like-minded Christian leaders in the National Council of Churches, could make such a suggestion to President Eisenhower and our State Department immediately."

*The Methodist Reporter's* news service was later discontinued, but all such utterances are magnified, distorted and broadcast wherever they serve Red ends. An example of the automatic spreading of such intelligence is the prominence given to a *United Press* quotation from a television interview with United States Senator Mike Mansfield, Democrat of Montana. Casual though his remark may have been, it was scattered over Latin America below two-column front page headlines in the English section and a five-column headline in the Spanish section of *The Americas Daily* of January 8, 1957.

Calling attention to the importance of Mansfield's position as a member of the Senate Committee on Foreign Relations, the dispatch, dated Washington, January 7, quoted the Senator as having said. "The United States could very well start to think about the internationalization of the Panama Canal." Further it said the Montana Senator "affirmed that in his opinion the Canal should be put under the control of the United Nations, 'as nobody can ever say when another Nasser may appear."

Senator Mansfield later explained to a constituent that he only said the suggestion of internationalization of the Panama Canal "might be worthy of study" and that he "did not advocate either approval or opposition."

The frightening seriousness of the internationalization threat was recognized by Senator John Marshall Butler, of Maryland, in a notable address to the Propeller Club of the United States, a national organization of shipping men, at their meeting in Washington on May 22, 1957 He referred to a leftist editor's advocacy of internationalization of the Panama Canal as a "dangerous brand of naive idealism" which "must not be allowed to gain the upper hand in the conduct of our international affairs. I will even go further and say that if the United States internationalizes the Panama Canal it will sign the death warrant for the entire Western Hemisphere."

Senator Butler further said. "It is an established fact that it is a fundamental object of Soviet Russian foreign policy to place the Panama Canal under communist control.... The key to the control of Central and South America — and eventually the United States — is the Panama Canal. If that waterway can be wrested from American control, communist infiltration into this hemisphere would be manifestly simple The proposal [to place the Canal under the United Nations, with Soviet veto power] should it be carried out, would place the right hand of International Communism at the very throat of the Western Hemisphere."

*Chapter 15*

# Isthmian Uproar Redoubled

The time-bomb planted by Alger Hiss in the United Nations in 1946 branding the Panama Canal Zone as an "occupied territory" became, by 1957, a regular implement for agitation by Panamanian politicians. If they could not get more concessions from Uncle Sam every time they demanded more, they could take their complaints to the United Nations.

Representative Daniel .J Flood, Democrat of Wilkes-Barre, Pennsylvania, member of the House Appropriations Committee and of its sub-committee for the Panama Canal, brought the Panamanian agitation to the attention of Congress on April 17, and again on May 29, 1957 In part he said:

"The diplomatic negotiations with Panama over a number of years have been featured by steady surrenders to that Republic of rights granted to the United States in the 1903 treaty Despite the very great advantages that accrued to Panama from the 1955 treaty, a so-called International Round Table Conference on Interoceanic Canals recently met at Panama with the apparent purpose of further liquidation of the rights of the United States as to the control and protection of the Panama Canal....

"During recent weeks much has been published about demands in Panama and other parts of Latin America for denunciation of the perpetuity clauses of the Hay-Bunau-Varilla Treaty, along with claims for increased annuity and other benefits, which must be borne either by the United States or by shipping that pays tolls, or both .

"All careful students of the Isthmian question know that the entire independence of Panama grew out of and is based on the Panama Canal. The economic life of that country, in large measure, depends on the Canal enterprise and, with the passage of the years, this dependence will probably increase

"Agitation about the Panama Canal has long been insidious and thus obscured to the public view, but now it is in the open. Conforming to the objectives of the communist conspiracy to place the United States on the defensive, it is aimed at the Panama Canal for the purpose of wresting its ownership from the United States. Thus the situation created by this propaganda is fraught with diplomatic danger and uncertainty to which the United States must be alert....

"The surrenders in the 1936 and 1955 treaties together with other relinquishments have served unfortunately to place the United States in a position without diplomatic bargaining power As was clearly foreseen by competent students of the subject, who, as far as I can determine, were not consulted in the course of the negotiations, these surrenders could only lead to new demands by Panama for further liquidation of the canal enterprise, the urgings for which are now being loudly voiced.

"Yet, our national administration remains strangely silent on this subject, and sinister propaganda affecting the future of the Panama Canal is having its full and unrefuted play."

Representative Flood urged Congress to act upon legislation first proposed in 1953 by Representative, later Senator, Thomas E. Martin, Republican of Iowa, and Representative Clark W Thompson, Democrat of Texas, and later sponsored by Representative Francis E Dorn, Republican of New York, and by Representative Flood, himself. Its purpose was to create an independent Interoceanic Canals Commission to make a thorough-going investigation of all engineering and diplomatic problems affecting the Panama Canal.

Congress delayed action, but Panama immediately took up Representative Flood's challenge. By this time Ricardo M. Arias, grand-nephew of Tomas Arias of the original Revolutionary Junta of 1903, had filled out the Presidency between Guizado's removal, 13 days after the Remon assassination of January 2, 1955, and the inauguration of Ernesto de la Guardia Jr, October 1, 1956, as Panama's twenty-sixth President Ricardo Arias was now Panama's Ambassador to Washington. Presumably voicing President de la Guardia's views, Arias in a letter to the *Washington Evening Star*, April 30, 1957, said.

"We have maintained, still maintain and shall continue to maintain that, because we enjoy sovereign rights over the Canal Zone, and have granted the United States only a restricted jurisdiction for certain specific purposes, the United States could not, under any circumstances, sell, transfer, or lease that territory as if it enjoyed the rights of sovereignty over it."

Representative Flood restated in his address of May 29, 1957, the juridical basis of United States relations with the Republic of Panama Then, on June 26, 1957, he introduced House Concurrent Resolution 205, and throughout the 1958 session of Congress urged its adoption. In this he was supported by resolutions of the American Legion Department of the Panama Canal and the national convention in Washington of the Daughters of the American Revolution.

"Resolved by the House of Representatives (the Senate concurring),

That (1), it is the sense and judgment of the Congress that the United States should not, in any wise, surrender to any other government or authority its jurisdiction over, and control of, the Canal Zone, and its ownership, control, management, maintenance, operation, and protection of the Panama Canal in accordance with existing treaty provisions; and that (2) it is to the best interests — not only of the United States, but, as well, of all nations and peoples — that all the powers, duties, authority, and obligations of the United States in the premises be continued in accordance with existing treaty provisions."

Representative Vincent J. Dellay of New Jersey, a member of the House Committee on Merchant Marine and Fisheries, joined the supporters of the Flood Concurrent Resolution 205 by introducing its identical text on July 31, 1958. Action on the Flood proposal was left over for the next Congress in 1959.

Representative Flood emphasized in his frank discussions of Panamanian problems in 1957, and again in 1958, his personal and official interest in maintaining friendly relations between the United States and Panama. "Questions at variance between the two countries," he said, "can be settled better by the two nations at the authorized council table rather than as a result of any effort by either country to pressure the other through processes of international propaganda."

Panamanian radicals, through their Spanish language press, answered with torrents of abuse, and anti-United States propaganda was intensified. The communist technique of inciting student rebellion was turned on full force against the conservative de la Guardia regime. On the night of July 24, 1957, Panamanian National Guard troops were used to break up a mob of some 2,000 who marched against police headquarters in Panama after Vice President Temistocles Diaz, feuding with the President, had addressed a three-hour political rally. The mob adopted resolutions demanding the President's immediate resignation.

Ten of the demonstrators were jailed, but the mob violence did not alter President de la Guardia's policy of moderation. He would not ask for more treaty revisions, nor suggest that his government should take over the Panama Canal. From his background of education in the United States and his success in business in Panama he realized that his country was not equipped to run the Canal. He would press for more "benefits," which would mean a still larger share of Canal tolls. And he moved to pacify the opposition by urging the United States to hasten implementation of the Eisenhower-Remon Treaty.

Again using the General Assembly of the United Nations as sounding-board, Panama's Foreign Minister, Aquilino E. Boyd, made headlines in Latin America — although scarcely noticed in the North American press — by this declaration on October 2, 1957: "Panama has insisted, periodically and through direct negotiations, on the revision of the terms that regulate our relations with the United States with reference to the Panama Canal." Minister Boyd added that international pacts, whether multilateral or unilateral, "should be revised according to changed relations."

Instead of dying down, the Isthmian uproar was redoubled on December 16, 1957, at the Second Congress of Students in the city of Panama through the voice of Ernesto Castillero, then Vice Minister of Foreign Relations and later Professor of Diplomacy at the University of Panama. Castillero was a leader of the so-called Student Movement, which started in Panama in 1943. Castillero told the Student Congress that the Eisenhower-Remon Treaty of 1955 fell far short of Panama's expectations and hopes. He reasserted Panama's "titular sovereignty" over the Canal Zone and declared that Panama should receive one-half of the gross income of the Canal enterprise.

President de la Guardia said Castillero's 50/50 division of

gross income was "not too realistic," but the Student Congress adopted resolutions calling on their government to negotiate with the United States for 50/50 sharing of the Canal's income. This was to be only an immediate objective; later they would fight until "our glorious national emblem flies with all its sovereign majesty over the Panama Canal."

This manipulation of student emotions — a process in world-wide use by the communist conspiracy — made headline news for anti-American papers in Panama and was well advertised in Latin America. Vice President Nixon was to experience its repercussions on his South American tour in 1958

Ambassador Arias further expounded the theme of Panamanian sovereignty over the Canal Zone in lecturing before the Foreign Service School of Georgetown University in Washington, April 29, 1958. There he disclosed a further ambition of Panama to demand treaty revision by which the United States would formally recognize Panama's absolute sovereignty over the Canal Zone

"Since 1904," said Ambassador Arias, "the people of Panama have been wishing for a fundamental revision of their relations with the United States . The foreign policy of my country during the last fifty years has been to exert every effort to obtain for Panama conditions similar to those granted by the United States to Colombia in January of 1903 . I am sure that in the end Panama will attain her purpose."

(The rejected Hay-Herran Treaty recognized "the general sovereignty of Colombia" over the proposed Canal Zone and permitted administrations by joint tribunals. William Nelson Cromwell's hand in drafting that treaty I have covered briefly in Chapter II.)

Again, on September 18, 1958, Panama's sovereignty ambition was expounded in the General Assembly of the United Nations by Aquilino Boyd's successor as Panama's Foreign Minister, Miguel J. Moreno:

"Under an agreement of 1903 my country conferred

upon the United States certain juridical powers over one part of our territory for one specific purpose, namely, the construction, maintenance, and protection of an interocean canal. Panama retains its sovereignty in that area, as it does throughout the rest of the territory of the Republic, and that sovereignty has never been the subject of renunciation

"I should like to make it clear that the Panamanian nation wishes to receive all the economic benefits to which it is entitled by reason of the operation of the Panama Canal, which is on the territory of our Republic"

Tragic reflexes of these sovereignty manifestoes made 1958 a memorable year in Isthmian history.

*Chapter 16*

# "*Operation Sovereignty*"

"Operation Sovereignty" was the 1958 headline-making title of Panamanian radicals' continuing campaign against the United States. Ostensibly a demonstration by high school and university students, the back-stage direction was at least in part communist. Fuel for this flame was poured out by Deputy Aleman, chairman of the Foreign Relations Committee of the National Assembly, in asserting that even the $1,930,000 annuity does not give Panama a "fair share" of Panama Canal revenues.

The student agitation started on May 2 with the planting of Panamanian flags — some accounts said 51, others 72 — at various strategic places in the Canal Zone, one in front of the Administration Building of the Canal Zone government. The raid was so "spontaneous" that Panamanian newspaper photographers were on hand to spread locally and as far away as Soviet Russia the visual proof of "Uncle Sam's humuliation"

Inconceivable as it was, the Canal Zone police made no

arrests. United States authorities said the incident should be ignored, but had the flags collected and returned to Panamanian officials, who handed them back to the students. And the students, emboldened by their escape from punishment or reprimand, marched with their flags on the Presidential Palace in Panama on the evening of May 5, 1958, and demanded that President de la Guardia take immediate steps to force recognition of Panamanian sovereignty over the Canal Zone He appeased the students by promising to ask that the Panamanian flag be flown in the Canal Zone. But this was not enough.

The political opposition then converted the student disorders into a campaign to overthrow the de la Guardia administration. Amidst scenes of wild disorder the students marched on the National Palace Their ultimatum to President de la Guardia was that he dismiss his Minister of Education, Victor N Juliao, and the three commanding officers of the Panama National Guard When this was refused, the students and their non-student communist allies tangled with the Guardsmen on May 19, 1958 One student was killed and 42 of them were counted among the 62 injured, who included 18 Guardsmen and two bystanders. Rioting spread to Colon on May 20 National Guard headquarters there were stormed with stones and bottles. Six Guardsmen and two children were injured.

The Student Federation decreed a 48-hour strike, whereupon President de la Guardia ordered the schools closed After six days of street fighting and bloodshed, window-shattering, bridge-burning, paralysis of business and transportation, eight killed and some 70 wounded, and a state of siege enforced, the President claimed a "decisive victory" for his policy of moderation. He would meet with the student leaders and a mediation committee headed by the Rector of Panama University

Net result of "Operation Sovereignty" and continued student rioting was the "voluntary" resignation of the de la Guardia cabinet Then the students were partially placated by the replacing of Minister of Education Juliao by Carlos Sucre, who was one of the negotiating team for the Eisenhower-Remon Treaty of 1955. The student demand for the scalps of the three chiefs of the National Guard was met by compromise, but this was deferred until the National Assembly met in October, 1958, and President de la Guardia presented a bill to limit the term of National Guard commanders to the incumbency of the President who appoints them.

This promised compromise did not prevent another student uproar in July, 1958, when Dr. Milton S. Eisenhower, official fact-finder for his brother, President Eisenhower, visited Panama for three days. Conspicuously guarded because of the attacks on Vice President Nixon in Lima and Caracas in May, Dr Milton Eisenhower twice rejected the students' invitation to meet them on their grounds They refused to visit him in the United States Embassy They merely picketed the Embassy with such signs as "50% of the Canal," "Milton Go Back to the U S A " and "Panama Canal for Panamanians."

Dr Eisenhower conferred at length with President de la Guardia and members of his Cabinet The Panamanian communique issued after the conference mentioned among the issues raised by the Panamanians "creation of a better moral climate of cooperation between the peoples of Panama and the United States" and "the flag of Panama in the Canal Zone and adoption of Spanish as the official language in the Canal Zone."

The student agitators were more aggressive in their demands If Dr Milton Eisenhower had allowed himself to be forced into a conference, they would have told him that "fundamental revision" of existing treaties between the United States and Panama would have been of first importance Their published list of "minimum aspirations" included the following:

"1. Express reaffirmation by the United States of the sovereignty of the Republic of Panama over the Canal Zone territory.

"2. Liquidation of the Panama Canal Company. [the U.S. Government corporation operating the Panama Canal] because it is a violation of the terms of existing treaties between the two countries.

"3. Substitution of the term 'in perpetuity' in the 1903 Canal Treaty by a period which will be in keeping with the principles of international law

"4. Sharing on an equality basis of economic benefits resulting from the Canal enterprise.

"5. Express recognition of Panama's civil, penal, fiscal and labor jurisdiction over non-military affairs in the Canal Zone.

"6. Elimination of discriminatory policies in the Canal Zone.

"7. The free use by Panama of the terminal ports of Balboa and Cristobal.

"8. Enforcement in the Canal Zone of the principle of equal pay for equal work.

"9. Preferential use of the Canal Zone market for Panamanian industry and commerce Elimination of private commercial companies in the Canal Zone.

"10. Raising of the Panamanian flag in the Canal Zone and recognition of Spanish language as official language.

"11. Elimination of United States postage stamps and exclusive use of Panamanian postal service in the Canal Zone

"12. Refund of the rentals collected by the United States on land formerly owned by the Panama Railroad Co"

A supplementary list of questions which the students said they hoped to discuss with Dr Eisenhower included.

"6. Cessation of provocative and offensive acts on the part of Canal Zone residents and members of Congress of the United States against national dignity"

"7. Ratification of the stand of the National Congress of Students for the nationalization of the Canal" [by the Republic of Panama]

Student agitators continued their campaign after the Milton Eisenhower visit and intensified their attacks on the de la Guardia administration. National Guardsmen nipped a revolutionary plot in the western province of Chiriqui in September, 1958, but the Student Federation countered by serving a four-day strike notice just ahead of the convening of the National Assembly From the pattern of endemic discord, pictured by the Panamanian press in day-to-day accounts of strikes and strike-threats, a note of caution was sounded in *La Nacion,* organ of the opposition. *La Nacion* was established in 1944 and is credited with the largest circulation of any Panamanian daily — 25,000 Its Director is Temistocles Diaz, who was Vice President in the early part of the de la Guardia term. In the October 3 issue of the *Daily Digest* of news and editorial opinion of Spanish language newspapers in Panama, issued in the Canal Zone, appeared this summary.

LA NACION, October 2

A column in *La Nacion* reports that today's youth should know a little more of Panama's history, particularly about those individuals who now clamor for the peaceful solving of the country's problems. Two of these individuals, who are now Presidential advisers, at one time were plotters of the greatest conspiracy in Panama's political history. One still carries the marks of his attempt to murder Belisario Porras and the other still may carry the bitter memory of his trial for high treason to his country; the latter once asked for intervention of U S. troops stationed in the Canal Zone. Among the student youth there is none who have thought of either of these two monstrous ideas.

o o o

A summary record of Panama's political instability, gleaned from authoritative sources by Representative Daniel J Flood, was included in his address to the House on April 2, 1958 For history's sake it is reprinted here from the *Congressional Record,* with two additional items set within brackets.

"November 14, 1904· Seditious and mutinous conduct

of the army of Panama (now National Police), with discovery of a plot to arrest President Amador, which was averted by diplomatic representations of the United States to preserve constitutional order as provided by treaty and the constitution of Panama

"October 11, 1925 Riot in Panama City with one person killed, 11 wounded, requiring assistance by United States Army to quell

"January 2, 1931. Revolution in Panama, requiring intervention of the United States Minister to save lives of Panamanian officials and the President, who were held prisoners, and resulting in the enforced resignation of the President.

"November 22, 1940 National Assembly adopted new constitution proposed by President Arnulfo Arias.

"October 9, 1941 Bloodless revolution ousted President Arias and installed Ricardo Adolfo de la Guardia as Provisional President.

[Arnulfo Arias was accused of making Panama a base for pro-Hitler propaganda and obstructing United States preparations for defense of the Panama Canal. He was imprisoned temporarily in Panama and allowed to go into exile in Managua. Former President Ricardo J Alfaro, an exile from the Arnulfo Arias dictatorship, in a public statement in New York in June, 1940 said "Democratic government has ceased to exist in Panama. It is an outright obligarchy. Trickery and courrpution had fixed things so that the Government party alone was represented at the voting booths. In the assaults against suffrage and the rights of the people, clubs, bayonets, machine guns and overcrowded jails got the upper hand."]

"Late 1944. Suspension of constitution caused 14 Panamanian Assemblymen to flee to the Canal Zone

"June 15, 1945 Constituent Assembly met, received resignation under duress of de la Guardia as Provisional President and elected Enrique A Jimenez as his successor.

"December 1, 1945· Armed revolt, for which former

President Arnulfo Arias was thrown into prison charged with participation. He was acquitted on July 29, 1946

"March 1, 1946: Constituent Assembly approved new constitution replacing the totalitarian instrument of Arnulfo Arias.

[November 14, 1946. Ricardo J Alfaro, as chairman of Panama's delegation to the United Nations, told the Trusteeship Committee of the UN General Assembly Panama retained its sovereignty over the Panama Canal Zone.]

"December 22, 1947 In the midst of disorder, National Assembly unanimously rejected a defense base treaty with the United States

"February 1948. United States announced withdrawal of all troops from military bases in the Republic as a consequence of the indicated rejection, and at considerable financial loss.

"July 28, 1949: First Vice President Daniel Chanis, Jr. succeeded ailing President Domingo Diaz Arosemena, on latter's resignation

"November 18, 1949· President Chanis accused Colonel Jose Remon, Chief of Police, of operating illegal monopolies, and dismissed him.

"November 20, 1949· President Chanis was forced to resign under pressure of National police headed by Remon, and Vice President Roberto F Chiari was sworn in as President.

"November 22, 1949. National Assembly voted for reinstatement of Chanis as President.

"November 24, 1949· Supreme Court upheld the claim of Chanis, but with support of national police former President Arnulfo Arias again became President on the contention of his sponsors that at the preceding election he had in fact defeated his opponent, Diaz, whose election had been officially declared, followed by his assumption of the Presidency.

"November 25, 1949· United States suspended relations

with Panama because of overthrow of 'constituted authorities'

"November 26, 1949. Chanis and two other former Presidents fled to Canal Zone to escape arrest

"December 14, 1949 United States recognized the Arnulfo Arias regime.

"May 7, 1951· President Arnulfo Arias decreed suspension of the constitution and dissolution of the National Assembly

"May 10, 1951. after bitter street fighting President Arnulfo Arias surrendered to Colonel Remon, Chief of National Police. Impeachment by National Assembly of President Arias and naming of First Vice President Alcibiades Arosemena as constitutional President resulted, and was upheld by Panama's Supreme Court

"October 1, 1951: Jose Antonio Remon inaugurated as President.

"January 2, 1955. President Remon assassinated.

"January 3, 1955. First Vice President Jose Ramon Guizado sworn in as President

"January 15, 1955. President Jose Ramon Guizado removed from office and placed under arrest charged with being implicated in assassination of President Remon."

Guizado was impeached, found guilty, and sentenced by the National Assembly to 10 years' imprisonment, of which he served only a portion and was released after all seven persons who were tried as principals, agents, or accessories to the Remon assassination were given jury acquittals.

o o o

The Republic of Panama credited in 1903 with a population of 262,300, now claims officially 1,000,000. A very small minority are of Spanish descent, the rest are native Indians and descendants of the thousands of West Indian Negroes who were brought in as laborers in Canal construction days. Another minority are an immigrant mixture from all parts of the earth attracted to the Isthmus as migrants were drawn to Suez in its early days.

The rising generation of Panamanians, ignorant of or misinformed about the history of the Caesarean operation that begot their Republic, seem not to realize that the Panama Canal never would have been built except for the stability of government guaranteed when the 1903 treaty placed perpetual and exclusive sovereignty over the Canal Zone in the United States.

All such agitation ignores the essential fact that the rights of the United States to the Canal Zone do not depend upon a terminable lease, as some misinformed people believe, but upon an *absolute grant* in the Hay-Bunau-Varilla Treaty — the birth certificate of the Panama Republic — signed November 18, 1903, ratified by Panama December 2, 1903, and made effective by exchange of ratifications in Washington February 26, 1904. The *grant, in perpetuity,* was bought and paid for by the $10,000,000 given by the United States to Panama, and the title has never been surrendered by the giveaway treaties of 1936-39 and 1955. The still indelible points of the 1903 treaty to be remembered are

ARTICLE II: The Republic of Panama *grants* to the United States *in perpetuity* the use, occupation and control of a zone of land and land under water for the construction, maintenance, operation, sanitation and protection of said Canal of the width of ten miles extending to the distance of five miles on each side of the center line of the route of the Canal to be constructed . with the proviso that the cities of Panama and Colon and the harbors adjacent to said cities .... shall not be included within this grant ...

ARTICLE III. The Republic of Panama grants to the United States all the rights, power and authority within the zone mentioned and described in Article II of this agreement .... which the United States would possess and exercise if it were the sovereign .... to the *entire exclusion* of the exercise by the Republic of Panama of any such sovereign rights, power or authority.

*Chapter 17*

# The Heritage of Conflict

Unless the United States gives away the Panama Canal it will have in the future to deal with today's Panamanian youth, who will have grown into Panamanian politicians. How are they to learn the truth about who created their Republic? Are North Americans willing to face up to their share of responsibility for the "tragedy of errors" that led to President Theodore Roosevelt's "taking" the Isthmus?

The history of the creation of the Republic of Panama will always be clouded with the conflicting personalities and contradictory assertions of two brilliant men, Cromwell and Bunau-Varilla. More should be recorded than can be compressed into a short book about the contradictions of these two extraordinary men, each credited largely or in part with the paternity of the Republic.

Bunau-Varilla died in Paris in 1940 at the age of 81, acclaimed there for having "engineered a revolution" to fulfill his boyhood dream of canal building in Panama. But in Panama his memory is reviled and he has been hanged in effigy by anti-Americans who say Bunau-Varilla negotiated

## The Heritage of Conflict

a treaty so good for the United States and so bad for Panama that he was guilty of a "great treason."

Cromwell died in New York in 1948 at the age of 94. Despite his grievance that the French Panama Canal Company's liquidators cut his bill for fees and disbursements from $832,449.38 to $228,282.71, he gave generously to the American Library in Paris, where he spent many of his later years. He told his French clients that his own time almost exclusively and much of his partners' had been devoted to Panama Canal matters for eight years and that consequently his firm had been compelled to turn away much lucrative law business. Still he left a fortune of $19,000,000.

*Who's Who in America* had no mention of Cromwell prior to its edition of 1903-05 Then it recorded:

CROMWELL, WILLIAM NELSON, lawyer; now senior of law firm of Sullivan & Cromwell, specialty is corporation law, organized, 1899, National Tube Co. (capital $80,000,000), since then many other corporations, appointed assignee and reorganized Decker, Howell & Co., 1890, and later Price, McCormick & Co., which had failed for several millions and put both on paying basis; officer, director or counsel of more than 20 other of the largest corporations in U S., including U S. Steel Corporation. Engaged by Panama Canal Co. of France and was instrumental in securing passage of Panama Canal bill in Congress, now engaged in perfecting details of the transfer of Panama Canal to U.S. Government.

In later editions of *Who's Who* appeared a list of some of Cromwell's corporate connections, including the various light and power companies from which it was known that he accumulated part of his vast fortune. Among them was his directorship in the Bowling Green Trust Company, through which dollars were siphoned to Panama to finance the "revolution." Several Panamanian patriots told me in 1910 they were certain it was Cromwell's guarantee, not Bunau-Varilla's, back of their borrowing $100,000 at the Bowling Green.

On his side of the ledger, Cromwell got for his French client escape from having to pay Colombia for permission to transfer to the United States its bankrupt canal diggings and its about-to-lapse concession. He succeeded in protecting the speculative profits of those who knew there was a "killing" to be made in the securities of the "Old" and the "New" Panama Canal companies who would have lost their share of whatever Colombia exacted for a transfer fee. And Cromwell made for himself the profitable job of managing the finances of the Infant Republic.

John Foster Dulles, now Secretary of State, was studying international law at the Sorbonne, Paris, 1908-09, when *The World* was seeking in vain to uncover in Paris the records of Cromwell's client, the French Panama Canal Company. Dulles began the practice of law in the Cromwell office in New York in 1911, became a partner in 1920 and senior partner in 1927. His younger brother, Allen W. Dulles, later to become Director of Central Intelligence Agency under the Executive Office of the President, was in the United States Foreign Service for ten years before joining the Cromwell firm in 1926.

In retrospect, Cromwell's manipulations contributed toward Theodore Roosevelt's thinking that as President he owed it to his country to do what he did, that it was morally right to support with armed force the Panama "revolution" and to be the dominant factor in setting up the Colombian province of Panama as the Panama Republic.

T.R. had been forearmed, as early as August, 1903, with a special memorandum by John Bassett Moore, eminent authority on international law, against the later accusation that his "taking" of the Isthmus was in violation of the treaty of 1846-48 with Colombia. Under that treaty, which was still in force in 1903, the United States *guaranteed* to Colombia (then called New Granada) the "rights of sovereignty over the said territory" — in return for the right of free transit across Colombia's Isthmus of Panama. The "Moore Memorandum" in effect held that the United States guaranteed

## The Heritage of Conflict

Colombia against attack by a foreign power but not against internal revolution. The Moore interpretation of the 1846-48 treaty, as well as Professor Moore's admitted assistance in preparing President Roosevelt's message to Congress in support of his action, loomed large in the controversy over eventual ratification of the Hay-Bunau-Varilla treaty, February 26, 1904.

Whether the United States did or did not directly and deliberately violate its treaty with Colombia, the fact will always remain that the United States did prevent Colombia from putting down the Panama "revolution." That fact unfortunately cost the United States the distrust and ill will of all of Latin America. Goodwill has been slowly and painfully regained, starting with the negotiation of the Thompson-Urrutia Treaty, signed in Bogota April 6, 1914, and resulting eventually in 1922 in the apologetic payment by the United States of $25,000,000 to Colombia. This was in partial reparation for Colombia's loss of territory and loss of income from the Panama Railroad and the Panama Canal. The Thompson-Urrutia Treaty recognized the title to Panama Canal facilities as vested in the United States.

Credit for the 1922 adjustment with Colombia belongs largely to the late James T. Du Bois, of Hallstead, Pennsylvania, a State Department veteran who was sent to Bogota as American Minister in 1911 to seek a way out of the impasse of America's refusal to submit the seizure of Panama to international arbitration. In a pamphlet published in 1914 Mr. Du Bois said:

> An impartial investigation at Bogota, running over a period of two years, convinced me that instead of 'blackmailers' and 'bandits' [T.R.'s characterization] the public men of Colombia compare well with the public men of other countries in intelligence and respectability . . .
> I deplore Colonel Roosevelt's bitter and misleading attack.... In the Panama incident, while doing what he believed to be a great thing for mankind and in accordance with the principles of the highest international mo-

rality, he did a bad thing for Colombia. He put himself in the position of a dentist apprentice who pulled the wrong tooth, he cannot put it back and he does not want his employer to realize his mistake...

Owing to the tender regard for ex-President Roosevelt contained in my instructions [from the Taft Administration] I failed  The Wilson Administration has taken a broader and more correct view of the entire question and has presented to the American people a treaty that ought to be heartily approved .   [The treaty was finally ratified under the Harding Administration in 1922 ]

I am a Republican and have been all my life, and I have been urged not to make this statement public because a successful issue of the treaty will help the Wilson Administration  I do not care to live to greet that day when my love of party smothers my love of justice and halts my courage in doing what I believe is right for the true interests of my country.

It will take courage of equally high degree to face up to the multiple dangers that threaten the future of the Panama Canal

Propaganda for wresting control of the Panama Canal from the United States and giving the Canal to the United Nations is far-reaching and persistent, with articulate spokesmen even in the United States

Clamor of misguided intellectuals and communist stooges for nationalization of the Canal by the Republic of Panama is too serious to be yawned off by apathetic ignorance.

And a continuing problem, too little understood by United States taxpayers, who own the Canal, or by its Panamanian beneficiaries, involves both engineering and politics. Modernization of the Panama Canal and consideration of a possible alternative waterway via Nicaragua and Costa Rica should not be neglected any longer by the United States Congress

*Chapter 18*

# Navigable Lake Canal vs. Sea-Level at Panama

Reform does not grow as rapidly as vegetation in the tropics Congressional committees on endless inspections of the machinery of the Panama Canal have ordered reforms, and then worried over the slowness of their accomplishment. Little has the taxpaying public realized that a tangle of conflicting authority and bureaucratic immobility grew up in the Canal Zone and became a perfect cover for engineering, administrative and diplomatic blundering.

Congress finally ordered a complete new setup as of July 1, 1951. Canal management was turned over to the Panama Canal Company, a new government-owned corporation. Other Canal Zone functions were left to the Canal Zone Government, headed by a Governor who "traditionally" has been an Army engineer. The Governor is also President of the Panama Canal Company.

"Traditional" also was the succession — an understudy of the Big Boss stepping into his shoes That line of succession was broken in 1952 when General John S. Seybold, who had not served in the Canal organization, was appointed Governor by President Truman.

Duplication of services and facilities, extravagance and waste persisted after Congress ordered reforms The Comptroller General of the United States in an audit report to Congress printed in July, 1954, said: "It is apparent that the Armed Services are reluctant to relinquish control over their activities " The Comptroller General recommended to Congress —

> that the Panama Canal Company and the Canal Zone Government be combined into a single independent government agency... that the organization be administered by a single *civilian* administrator or by a small *civilian* board or commission composed of not more than three members....
>
> The administrator or members of the board should serve *full time, reside in the Canal Zone,* and be selected on the basis of successful backgrounds in governmental, utility, and commercial fields .
>
> The number of improvements during the past year has been limited because most of the board members (of the government-owned Panama Canal Company) have outside interests in the United States requiring practically all of their time and attention.

Examples of bungling and waste cited in the Comptroller General's audit reports to Congress in recent years, if disclosed in a business enterprise, would drive stockholders to fire the management But Army engineers continue to run the show at Panama. They have made and are still making improvements, subject to periodic checkups by Congressional committees and some guidance by the Panama Canal Company's board of nonresident and part-time directors.

Unwatched bureaucracies everywhere are susceptible to the viruses of Makeshift and Squandermania Neither tropical climate nor distance from home minimized the virulence of these germs on the Isthmus

*Makeshift* overtook the Panama Canal early in the planning period, when haste to "make the dirt fly" brought political pressures to bear on engineering judgment. John F. Stevens, Chief Engineer, 1905-07, was belatedly recognized in a memorable address by Representative Flood before the Panama Canal Society of Washington, D.C., May 12, 1956, as "the basic architect" of the Canal. Stevens would have avoided making an operational bottleneck at the Pacific end of Gatun Lake, where lack of anchorage space has been a costly handicap to ship transit He would have avoided this by extending Gatun Lake to Miraflores and building there a triple set of locks instead of one at Pedro Miguel and two at Miraflores. Modernization of the Canal, long overdue and now urgently needed, is facing this bottleneck as one of its problems

*Squandermania,* the companion of Makeshift, has been far from idle on the Canal Its greatest single exploit, so far, has been the spending of $75,000,000 toward building a third set of locks, authorized in 1939, started in 1940, abandoned in May, 1942 One of the undisclosed and unauthorized objectives of the third-locks program was eventual conversion of the Canal to a "sea-level strait," although the sea-level problems had not been comprehensively investigated The French dreamed of a "sea-level" canal and abandoned it as impracticable with equipment then available. But the idea has been a "hardy perennial" — so described by J. J. Morrow, Canal Zone Governor in the early 1920's.

To find the roots of the $75,000,000 third-locks fiasco one must dig back to the Interoceanic Canal Board's study of 1929-31. This was largely administrative in its original concept, but eventually it evolved into makeshift plans for a third set of locks to increase temporarily the canal's capacity pending conversion to sea-level. This was to be followed some time in the future by construction of a second American canal through Nicaragua.

A basic defect of the 1929-31 "study" by the Panama Canal planners raised many eyebrows among shipping men.

Not one of the members of the planning board had had navigational experience. All were engineers. What they knew, except on paper, about marine operating problems may have been buried in the abandoned $75,000,000 holes dug for the third locks, which were estimated to cost $277,000,000 if they could have been completed at costs then prevailing.

World War II brought overwhelming traffic problems incident to the transit of naval vessels through the canal. Out of this necessity grew the first major proposal for operational improvement of the canal since John F. Stevens, in 1906, and Colonel William L. Sibert, in 1908, were overruled when they proposed to avoid the Pedro Miguel bottleneck by consolidating the two sets of Pacific locks at Miraflores.

Born of war's necessities and the application of navigational experience to the major problems of the Panama Canal, a new proposal — to become known as the Terminal Lake-Third Locks Plan — was developed by Commander Miles P. Duval, U S N , Captain of the Port, Balboa, Canal Zone The plan was presented in detail before the Panama Section, American Society of Civil Engineers, at Balboa College, Canal Zone, May 20, 1943.

Eventually the Terminal Lake-Third Locks Plan was forwarded by the Secretary of the Navy to President Franklin Delano Roosevelt on September 7, 1943. But the plan did not become public until presented in the February, 1947, issue of the American Society of Civil Engineers Proceedings — an "untold story" for almost four years.

Meanwhile the impact of the atomic bomb in 1945 led the Canal organization to draft and present to Congress a bill to authorize the Governor of the Panama Canal (now called Governor of the Canal Zone) to make a comprehensive investigation of the means for increasing the Canal's capacity *and security* to meet the future needs of interoceanic commerce and *national defense*. The law, as approved December 28, 1945, provided also for a restudy of the abandoned third locks project, for a study of possible canals at other locations, and for consideration of any new means for transporting ships across land.

Then, by the simple device of emphasizing the *security* and *national defense* factors which they had put into the draft of their bill before sending it to Congress, the Brass Hats in the Canal organization were able to interpret the law as a *mandate* of Congress to favor a sea-level canal as "less vulnerable" than the Terminal Lake-Third Locks solution. This alleged "mandate," say informed members of Congress, was never intended to be mandatory. Later revelations clearly established that sea-level was the pre-determined objective of the investigators then in control.

The main argument of sea-level planners was that their type of canal would be safer under A-or-H bomb attack, no matter how much the Canal could be modernized under the Terminal Lake-Third Locks Plan. The validity of the sea-level "security" claims has been challenged repeatedly in and out of Congress by engineers with canal building experience and by naval and military experts.

To a layman, this is a natural question: Would giving the Panama Canal to the United Nations make it any more secure? Representative Flood answered in Congress on April 17, 1957:

> "In the event of war the forces of world communism would in no wise respect the neutrality of the Canal, whether under Panamanian or international control. They would certainly seek to destroy it as a matter of their war strategy, which is characterized by unfailing defiance of every concept of freedom and international law."

Representative Willis W. Bradley of California, a retired naval officer and recognized Congressional leader in studying canal problems, attacked the sea-level fallacies. "As far as I can ascertain," he said, "the greatest authorities on modern weapons of war who have given this subject serious attention hold uniformly that any canal would be critically vulnerable to the atomic bomb, regardless of type, that a sea-level canal would be in the same security class as a lake canal, that a sea-level canal could be closed for prolonged periods beyond any hope of speedy restoration, and that a sea-level canal cannot be considered secure in an atomic war. These same authorities also agree that the atomic bomb is irrelevant as a controlling factor in the planning of operational improvements for the Panama Canal."

Among the experts who early spoke up against the sea-level project were Major General Thomas F Farrell, who was inside the atomic and thermonuclear developments since their beginning, and E Sydney Randolph, consulting engineer of Baton Rouge, La., who spent 35 years on Panama Canal construction and operation

General Farrell wrote to Senator Martin. "Atomic and thermonuclear weapons —if delivered on the target — will put a sea-level canal out of service as effectively as they would a lock canal."

Representative Francis E Dorn of New York, himself a close student of Panama Canal problems, put in the *Congressional Record* of April 18, 1956, a statement by Canal Engineer Randolph.

"The sea-level plan," said Randolph, "contains engineering and constructional features which are grossly without precedent in the Isthmian area . . . The oversize dredging equipment required for deepening the cut before lowering the water level would necessitate a program of development involving unforeseeable risks, delays and costs."

Any layman could deduce from this that the sea-level project would be a veritable bottomless pit.

"Without experience," continued Randolph, "There is no solid basis for the evaluation of the action of materials under the new order of pressures which would be developed. [by deepening the canal 108 feet from its present height to bring it down to sea-level]The problem of land slides would be greatly accentuated . . .

"The interoceanic canal problem includes, besides engineering and geology, grave questions of diplomatic relationships, economics, and marine operations. The issues must be decided on their merit at the highest plane of wise and experienced judgment and statesmanship This I firmly believe can be best accomplished by an independent and broadly constituted commission "

The Terminal Lake-Third Locks Plan was approved in principle by the then Governor, General Glen E. Edgerton, in his report to the Secretary of War, January 17, 1944 This report was previously "classified" and did not reach the public until Senator Martin obtained, by request, a copy from Assistant Secretary of War George H. Roderick and placed the complete text of the Edgerton Report in the *Congressional Record*, June 21, 1956 Here was an official admission of the pre-determined objective of the sea-level planners as far back as 1944. The following is from paragraph 70 of the Edgerton Report.

> "It is possible that advocates of a sea-level canal would oppose *unjustifiably* any expensive change in present plans on the grounds that it would defer the time when the conversion of the existing canal to a sea-level waterway might otherwise be authorized "

Sea-level partizans did not need to use "unjustifiable" arguments Public hysteria over atomic bomb developments came at the right time to serve their purpose. Emphasis upon *security* and *national defense* was enough to influence the uninformed The argument was that the addition of a few billion dollars to the cost of the Canal could be charged to national defense — a burden on all United States taxpayers. If this idea could be put over, the shipping industry would escape payment of still higher canal tolls which, otherwise, must result from increasing the capital investment in the canal by the $2,483,000,000 which the planners initially estimated would be the cost of sea-level at prices prevailing in 1947.

But the sea-level planners' report met a cold reception

when President Truman sent the Canal Governor's document to Congress on December 1, 1947. No Presidential approval, no comment, no recommendation went with it. Congress, unimpressed, took no action on it. Instead, Congress authorized in 1949 its own investigation of the entire Canal organization. Representative Clark W. Thompson, Democrat of Texas, a retired Marine Corps Reserve officer, headed the committee of inquiry Its report resulted in the first basic change in the Canal operating organization since it was established in 1914 The new organization, dividing the Canal Zone Government and the new Panama Canal Company into a one-headed entity still run by Army engineers, was ordered by Congress to be a self-supporting enterprise.

Civilian engineers who helped build the canal challenged the sea-level planners' estimated cost of $2,483,000,000 as absurdly low, even under 1947 prices Some of them estimate the cost of a sea-level canal at Panama at possibly $10,000,000,000

The Panama sea-level project was advocated in 1956 by a private organization headquartered in New Orleans under the impressive title of "National Rivers and Harbors Congress" — a registered lobby organization That group, through a "special committee" of five members who signed an elaborately printed report, accepted the conclusions of the 1947 planners, but raised the estimate of the total cost of the project, as of March 30, 1956, to "approximately $4,879,000,000 "

And this would not include the incalculable cost of obtaining from the Government of Panama a new treaty to permit changes in Canal Zone boundaries required by construction at sea-level.

There was nothing in the report of the New Orleans "special committee" to indicate they made any investigation on the Isthmus, or that they ever worked on the Canal. Their report reads like a rewirte or a condensation of the sea-levelers' document of 1947.

A completely opposing view was expressed in a memorial signed in 1954 by fourteen old canal diggers and by John F Stevens, Jr., since deceased, who inherited his devotion to canal problems from his father, now remembered as the "basic architect" of the waterway The fifteen signers of the memorial urged Congress not to delay creating an independent commission to re-evaluate already available data. "Such a body," they told Congress, "should be made up of unbiased men of widest engineering, operational, governmental and business experience, and not persons from routine agencies, all too often involved in justifying their own groups"

The concern of old employees, from hospital nurses to chief engineers, for the future of the Panama Canal binds their thinning ranks into Panama Canal Societies that hold annual reunions in New York, Washington, Miami, Chicago and Los Angeles Once you have touched Panama, you never lose the infection Some call it "Canalitis."

William R. McCann, consulting engineer, retired from his executive functions in large American corporations, has poured out a continual stream of memoranda on current Panama developments to a great mailing list of officials and plain citizens who he thinks should be concerned over the Panama Canal lifeline

"The history of the Panama Canal since 1931," said McCann in one of his bulletins, "establishes that problems in major planning will not be properly resolved by routine Canal officials nor by harassed administrators in the executive departments who depend on Canal officials for advice"

Maruice H. Thatcher, member of the last Isthmian Canal Commission, Civil Governor of the Canal Zone, 1910-13, and Member of Congress from Kentucky, 1923-33, told me in 1956 that of all the engineers, then living, who had experience in building or operating the Canal, not one approved the Panama sea-level project. Further, on the threat of internationalization, Governor Thatcher told the 1956 meeting of the Panama Canal Society of Washington:

"There are those who wish to see the Panama Canal . . . . .turned over to an international or world organization which would, very likely, team up with the world-at-large and use it in a way to greatly harm this nation . . .

"There is no other country in all the earth which, if it had built the Canal as we have built it, would surrender its right to own, control, and operate it . . . .

"Yet there are those in our midst at this hour —at this time of grave danger to the freedom of the entire human race — who, through impractical idealism or sinister design, would yield up all these precious and dearly earned rights, which are ours . . . .

"Our abandonment of the control of this great waterway, beneficent and strategic, would be, indeed, an act of stupendous folly."

Opponents of internationalization of the Panama Canal through the United Nations or nationalization by the Republic of Panama should realize that sea-level advocates will be active as long as the door to limitless spending is not shut tight. Every spenders' lobby knows the procedure. It is notorious that government engineers habitually *underestimate* the cost of projects in which they are particularly interested. They get the job *started*, and then count on Congress to meet their deficits.

o o o

Fortunately for United States taxpayers, Congress, by the reorganization effective July 1, 1951, required the Panama Canal Company, as a government agency, to operate on a self-supporting basis. Under the administration of Major General William E. Potter, as President of the Panama Canal Company and Governor of the Canal Zone, the Canal at the end of the fiscal year 1958 completed seven successive years of operation, since the reorganization, without loss. During the seven-year period the Panama Canal Company has made capital repayments of $15 million to the United States Treasury, thereby reducing the Government's net direct investment in the Panama Canal, as of June 30, 1958, to $351,861,652.

The number of commercial ships now transiting the Canal has risen to the average of 25 2 per day. For 1958 the total of ocean-going ships passing through the Canal rose to 9,466 under the flags of some 36 nations The year's receipts from tolls rose 8 per cent to $42,834,006 But net revenue declined from $3,821,456 in 1957 to $2,656,382 in fiscal year 1958, due to a sharp rise in operating expenses primarily caused by wage increases. The Canal employs approximately 11,000.

The increasing size of commercial ships using the Canal has raised the average amount of tolls, per ship, from $4,127 in 1952 to $4,549 in fiscal year 1958 But bigger ships have added to Canal problems The number of ships using the Canal with a beam of 86 feet or more increased frm 13 in 1955 to 109 in 1958 The bigger ships cannot pass one another in the narrow channel of Gaillard (formerly Culebra) Cut This problem has grown by 56 per cent since 1955

Canal management research now indicates larger vessels and steadily increasing volume of trans-Isthmian cargo for the years ahead Estimates are that cargo volume will increase by 73 per cent by 1975 and 136 per cent by the end of the century

A long-range study of future requirements, authorized by the Board of Directors of the Panama Canal Company, is also under way. This "study" is based "on data already available in the Isthmian Canal Studies — 1947 Report," says the 1958 Annual Report of the Board of Directors The "data already available" can bring back to life the old controversy between lake and sea-level advocates.

While the United States Congress marked time on the long-pending Martin-Thompson-Flood bills to create a new Interoceanic Canals Commission to re-evaluate all trans-Isthmian problems, the House Merchant Marine Committee acted. Its Chairman, Representative Herbert C Bonner, Democrat of North Carolina, recognized the "approaching obsolescence" of the Panama Canal and "the need for additional facilities either in the Canal Zone or at alternate locations in the Central American Isthmus." Chairman Bonner appointed a special Board of Consultants to undertake what the sponsors of a full Congressional inquiry had planned.

The breadth of experience of the six consultants is reassuring to United States taxpayers. Their initial report, delivered to Chairman Bonner on July 15, 1958, covered only the short-range improvement program. Their recommendations were drafted after studying basic engineering data and cost estimates and the testimony of Governor Potter and others who appeared in Washington prior to the consultants spending five days inspecting facilities on the Canal Zone.

The personnel and experience of this Board of Consultants belong in any record of the Panama Canal's present and future.

S. C. Hollister, dean of the College of Engineering, Cornell University, Ithaca, N.Y. was elected Chairman by the other five From his early engineering experience on flood control projects in the Pacific Northwest, Dr. Hollister became a recognized consultant on major construction projects, including the Boulder Dam.

Lt. Gen. Leslie R. Groves, U.S.A Retired; wartime head of the Manhattan Project which developed the atomic bomb, as a young Army officer surveyed western end of projected Nicaragua Canal, 1929-31, Vice President, since 1948, of RemingtonRand Division of Sperry Rand Corporation.

E. Sydney Randolph, consulting engineer, Baton Rouge, La.; principal and consulting engineer on biggest construction and maintenance jobs on Panama Canal, 1910-46.

E. Hartley Rowe, electrical and construction engineer on Panama Canal 1910-15; then chief engineer and vice president of United Fruit Company, Boston, Mass , until retirement in 1957; now consulting engineer in Boston.

John E. Slater, member of consulting engineering firm of

Coverdale & Colpitts, New York City, and formerly President of American Export Lines.

Francis S. Friel, President of Albright & Friel, Inc. consulting engineers, Philadelphia, Pa., and vice president of the American Society of Civil Engineers.

The Consultants in their July 15, 1958 report to Chairman Bonner commended the progress made by the Canal management on its short-range improvement program. What they will advise on the long-range problems remained for later sessions.

At this writing, still unanswered are these questions.

1 Should the existing Panama Canal be modernized and its capacity expanded sufficiently to meet all foreseeable future needs by the Terminal Lake-Third Locks Plan — at economic cost?

2 Should the United States build a new Panama Canal at sea-level — at astronomical cost in dollars and diplomatic uncertainties?

3. Should an alternate Isthmian canal be undertaken, and when?

o o o

The Panama Canal's history has been featured by periodic crises and bewildering confusions Nowhere are comprehensively stated the broad principles of policy governing its operation and management. Yet over the years its main objectives have evolved "The best type of canal at the best site for the transit of vessels of commerce and war of all nations on terms of equality as provided by treaty — and at low cost of construction, maintenance, operation, sanitation, and protection."

Today the Isthmian waterway seems verging toward what may prove its greatest crisis — a crisis in which the problems of increased capacity and modernization are immeasurably complicated by organized attacks on United States jurisdiction and by widespread propaganda for predetermined objectives that entirely disregard costs and tolls.

Successive failures of routine administrative officials in planning acceptable solutions for modernization of the Panama Canal and for protection of United States interests in the Isthmian area have been repeatedly criticized by Committees of Congress Adoption of businesslike methods, urged by the Comptroller General of the United States and the Director of the Budget, has been a forward step

Finally, Congressional leaders, cognizant of the hazards and failures, secured authority, in House Resolution 149, adopted February 27, 1957, for a comprehensive inquiry into all aspects of the interoceanic canal problem. Out of this inquiry by the Board of Consultants, now only partially completed, United States taxpayers hope for a constructive reassessment of Isthmian canal problems and a program for their permanent solution which an informed Congress can approve and authorize.

*Chapter 19*

# Nicaragua-Alternative to Monopoly at Panama

Panama, by unanimous vote of its General Assembly, December 23, 1947, forced the United States to abandon its defense bases outside the Canal Zone — as detailed in Chapter XII Instant reaction in the United States was "Build another canal!"

Minor alternatives were suggested — in Colombia, via the Atrato River, in Mexico, across the Isthmus of Tehauntepec But informed opinion centered on the Nicaragua route, long considered the great alternative to Panama Anastasio Somoza, for many years the ruling chief of Nicaragua, promptly telephoned his offer of cooperation to press associations in the United States Whatever might be required for canal construction and for military bases to protect the canal would be made available.

*The New York Times* in its leading editorial of December 25, 1947, commended United States authorities for withdrawing from the defense bases. There was nothing else to do after Panama's National Assembly repudiated the already-signed agreement of its government to lease fourteen of the most important bases to the United States. *The Times* concluded

" .... the Panamanian action has also called sharp attention to the inadequacy of the Panama Canal itself. As it stands now, its security can always be imperiled by a purely local situation. Moreover, its locks are highly vulnerable to air attack in any case, and it has become too narrow for our modern warships.

"And that lends added importance to the long-standing proposal for a bigger and better sea-level canal across Nicaragua. The United States had planned to spend two and a half billion dollars on improving the present channel. It might be better to spend that money on a new seaway which would not only more than double the present facilities but would also immeasurably increase their security"

The powerful Gannett newspapers, January 1, 1948, published their cartoon of Uncle Sam standing beside the Canal accepting the defense sites rejection and saying blandly to little Mr Panama. "O K THEN, BROTHER, WE'LL MOVE!"

Still more emphatic were the Hearst newspapers, coast to coast They editorialized and reproduced cartoons they had published over the years depicting the insecurity of Uncle Sam carrying all his defense and commerce eggs in the one basket of Panama, when another basket, empty in the graphic mapping, lay across Nicaragua.

Reproduced, with editorial emphasis, was a letter written by the elder William Randolph Hearst, February 7, 1929, to Representative Loring M. Black, of New York, and preserved in the *Congressional Record*

"I have been advocating the Nicaragua route for nearly thirty-five years," wrote the founder of the Hearst press. "I advocated it first in preference to the Panama route because I thought it involved fewer engineering difficulties and fewer foundation problems, and because it provided for a better canal and a quicker route, and finally because it was more easily defended and less easily destroyed in time of war . . Now another canal is needed to accommodate constantly increasing Trans-Isthmian traffic .. "

In a full-page illustrated editorial, January 27, 1948, and again on February 26, 1948, the Hearst papers said in part:

"Years ago the Hearst newspapers perceived the folly of entrusting our security to the Panama Canal locks when a sea-level waterway across Nicaragua could be ours for the building  Now the facts have been belatedly recognized .  Our dormant right-of-way in Nicaragua is to be utilized at long last . . . . Under the Bryan-Chamorro Treaty we obtained absolute rights in Nicaragua

"The Nicaragua Canal, if built, would be accorded every facility for its defense by the Government of Nicaragua, which has proved itself utterly unreceptive to Communist infiltration and apparently unsusceptible to Communist propaganda. The Nicaragua Canal would be far more adequate for all foreseeable navigation needs than the Panama Canal, however the latter might be improved. It could be constructed at less cost than the Panama Canal could be improved, and it would be a shorter route between the two American seaboards.

"The case for the Nicaragua Canal has always been sound, and now it is complete, by virtue of the recent events [ Panama's refusal to lease defense bases] which have so amply clarified the situation."

The renewed anti-American agitation in Panama in 1957 prompted a "Let's Look Again" editorial in Hearst's *Los Angeles Examiner*·

"There have always been good and compelling reasons why a second intercoastal waterway should be built across Nicaragua . A newer problem, which may be more serious in the future than it is now, is that presented by the opportunists in Panama who are taking advantage of the controversy over the Suez Canal to propose nationalization of the Panama waterway. . . .

"Before spending billions to improve the Panama Canal, and still have an inadequate and obsolete waterway on our hands and still face the possibility of a nationalization campaign by unfriendly elements in Panama, a new and long look should be taken once more at the too-long delayed Nicaraguan project."

    ° ° °

The first essential to any intelligent look at the Nicaragua Canal project is a re-examination and interpretation of the Bryan-Chamorro Treaty of 1914 Ratification was voted by the United States Senate, February 18, 1916, with the proviso that Nicaragua's failure to consult Costa Rica before entering into a canal treaty with the United States should not invalidate Costa Rica's rights under the Costa Rica-Nicaragua Treaty of 1858, which gave Costa Rica veto power over a Nicaragua canal violating territorial rights or causing flood damage to Costa Rica's adjoining territory. One of the plans for a canal through Nicaragua makes Salinas Bay, in Costa Rican territory, its Pacific terminal port Costa Rica has long been friendly to canal projects

Another question is whether the Bryan-Chamorro Treaty grants even an enforceable option to the United States to build a canal. The representative of Nicaragua told the Central American Court of Justice that the Bryan-Chamorro Treaty "merely deals with a preferential right granted to the United States to open an inter-oceanic passageway through a route to be designated out of national territory when it shall be decided by agreement between the two governments to undertake the construction thereof, at which time the conditions under which the canal shall be constructed, operated, and maintained will be determined by a further treaty or convention between the contracting parties . . ."

Senator William F Knowland of California recognized the preliminary character of the Bryan-Chamorro Treaty in the bill he introduced in the Senate, January 7, 1948, for a canal through Nicaragua If passed, the Knowland bill would have requested the President to enter into negotiations with the Government of Nicaragua for a treaty "agreeing upon the details of the terms under which such canal shall be constructed, operated and maintained."

The complete text of Articles I and II of the Bryan-Chamorro Treaty belong in any discussion of Isthmian problems.

## Article I

"The Government of Nicaragua grants in perpetuity to the Government of the United States, forever free from all taxation or other public charge, the exclusive proprietary rights necessary and convenient for the construction, operation and maintenance of an interoceanic canal by way of the San Juan River and the great Lake of Nicaragua or by way of any route over Nicaraguan territory, the details of the terms upon which such canal shall be constructed, operated and maintained to be agreed to by the two governments whenever the Government of the United States shall notify the Government of Nicaragua of its desire or intention to construct such canal.

## Article II

"To enable the Government of the United States to protect the Panama Canal and the proprietary rights granted to the Government of the United States by the foregoing article, and also to enable the Government of the United States to take any measure necessary to the ends contemplated herein, the Government of Nicaragua hereby leases for a term of ninety-nine years to the Government of the United States the islands in the Caribbean Sea known as Great Corn Island and Little Corn Island, and the Government of Nicaragua further grants to the Government of the United States for a like period of ninety-nine years the right to establish, operate and maintain a naval base at such place on the territory of Nicaragua bordering upon the Gulf of Fonseca as the Government of the United States may select. The Government of the United States shall have the option of renewing for a further term of ninety-nine years the above leases and grants upon the expiration of their respective terms, it being expressly agreed that the territory hereby leased and the naval base which may be maintained under the grant aforesaid shall be subject exclusively to the laws and sovereign authority of the United States during the terms of such lease and grant and of any renewal or renewals thereof."

The third and final article of the Bryan-Chamorro Treaty, which became effective by exchange of ratifications in Washington, June 22, 1916, set forth the consideration agreed upon by the two governments It was payment to the Government of Nicaragua by the United States of $3,000,000 "to be applied by Nicaragua upon its indebtedness or other public purposes for the advancement of the welfare of Nicaragua in a manner to be determined by the two High Contracting Parties."

Members of the Board of Consulatnts advising the House Merchant Marine Committee have received, but at this writing have not reported upon, recommendations for a sea-level canal proposed by a private organization calling itself the Nicaraguan Strait Development Co., Inc. of Managua, Nicaragua It is headed by Carl Svarverud, a Californian, whose earlier interests were in mineral developments in Mexico.

The Svarverud proposal will be challenged by some experts because it would drain most of the area of Lake Nicaragua and cut a wide sea-level strait from Punta Gorda, on the east coast, where a harbor would have to be built, to Salinas Bay on the Pacific. Drainage of Lake Nicaragua is not a new idea. It was suggested to the International Geographical Congress in Paris in 1878. It would deprive some Nicaraguans of their accustomed lake transit, but would release vast areas for highly profitable cultivation — assuming that the drained areas would be the rich agricultural land that promoters of this plan assume it would be

The Svarverud sea-level plan was presented to the members of the Board of Consultants with maps and pictures of recently developed giant earth-moving equipment. Svarverud told them that the plan he proposes would result in a canal "twice as wide as the Panama Canal, six times as wide as the Panama Canal locks, twenty feet deeper," and, because of lower tide levels than at Panama, the Nicaragua sea-level strait, although more than three times as long as the 50-mile Panama crossing, would be easily navigable and would not require tide-locks, as a sea-level canal at Panama would require.

The giant earth-moving equipment now in use, according to the Svarverud proposal, would complete "within five years" the sea-level strait through Nicaragua "with a labor force of less than 10,000 men moving five billion cubic yards of earth in less than half the time it took a total labor force of about 40,000 men to excavate one-quarter billion cubic yards of earth and rock at Panama."

Like all other estimates, Svarverud's guess at total cost of a sea-level strait through Nicaragua is for consulting experts, not laymen, to appraise. This was his figure:

"A sea-level canal across Nicaragua at actual cost of construction, with the proper use of newly developed large-scale dirt moving and excavating equipment, could be built for between two and three billion dollars."

## RECOMMENDED READING

Abbott, Henry L. *Problems of the Panama Canal.* (2d ed.) New York Macmillan, 1907

Bennett, Ira E. *History of the Panama Canal.* Washington, D C Historical Publishing Co., 1915

Comptroller General of the Unied States. Reports on Audit of Panama Canal Company and Canal Zone Government, 1952 and subsequent years.

DuVal, Miles P., Jr. *Cadiz to Cathay.* Stanford, Calif. Stanford University Press, 1940

——*And the Mountains Will Move.* Stanford, Calif : Stanford University Press, 1947.

——"The Marine Operating Problems, Panama Canal, and the Solution." American Society of Civil Engineers *Transactions,* Vol 114 (1949), p. 558.

——"Isthmian Canal Policy — An Evaluation." United States Naval Institute *Proceedings,* Vol. 81 (Mar. 1955) p. 263.

Goethals, George W. *The Panama Canal; An Engineering Treatise.* McGraw-Hill Book Company, 1916. 2 volumes.

Hebard, R. W. *The Panama Railroad — The First Transcontinental,* 1855-1955. 415 Fifth Ave , New York.

Miner, Dwight C. *The Fight for the Panama Route.* New York· Columbia University Press, 1940.

Sands, William F and Joseph M. Lalley. *Our Jungle Diplomacy.* Chapel Hill, N. C · University of North Carolina Press, 1944, Chapter I

Stevens, John F *An Engineer's Recollections.* New York. McGraw-Hill Publishing Co, 1936.

Sibert, William L. and John F. Stevens. *The Construction of the Panama Canal.* New York. D. Appleton, 1915.

*Story of Panama.* "Hearings on the Rainey Resolution Before the Commitee on Foreign Affairs of the House of Representatives, January 26 and February 9, 12, 13, 14, 15, 16 and 20, 1912" Washington. Government Printing Office, 1912 Reprinted in 1913 with unsworn statement of Philippe Bunau-Varilla attacking the veracity of William Nelson Cromwell Both the 1912 and 1913 printings contain complete text of Cromwell's brief, or bill of particulars, supporting his claim for $832,449 38 for his services to the French Panama canal companies which Paris arbitrators reduced to $228,282.71

Stratton, James H. et al. "Panama Canal — Sea-level Project Symposium.' American Society of Civil Engineers *Transactions* (New York). Vol. 114 (1949), pp. 607-906. (Summary of report of the Governor of the Panama Canal under Public Law 280, 79th Congress, which report failed to receive Presidential approval and was not accepted by Congress.

Thompson, Hon Clark W "Isthmian Canal Policy of the United States — Documentation." *Congressional Record,* March 23, 1955. This is an invaluable listing of books and authors, magazine articles, editorials, official reports, speeches in and out of Congress throwing light from all sides on the problems of the Panama Canal.

Interoceanic Canal Board's study of 1929-31 appears in House Document 139, 72nd Congress.

# *Index*

## A

Abbot, Henry L, 172
Acheson, Dean 110
Albert, Charles S, 20
AFL, 106
Albright & Friel, 163
Alfaro, Ricardo J, 103, 109, 110, 142, 143
Alibis planned, 25, "I am sick, come," 25, Cromwell to Shaler, 27
Alienation of territory, 21
Alling, Robert B, 86
Amador Guerrero, Manuel, 23, 24, 35, 60 65, 89, his "Dear Little Son" letter, 73, his edited script, 75, his ambition to be first minister, 40, incensed by Bunau-Varilla, 41, his mental reservations, 75, 76, his estate, 77, saw T R in White House, 85, 86
Amador, Jenny Smith, 66, 86
Amador, Manuel E, 36, 67
Amador, Maria de la Ossa, 32, 33, 67, 76, bullied by Junta members, 77, saved the "revolution," 78, quoted in Havana, 78, her death in Charlottesville, 88
Amador, Marthe Lenoir, 88

Amador, Raoul A, 25, 40, 66, 67, 70, 71, 100, called "loco," 70, 72, his Waldorf luncheon, 74, his father's manuscript, 75, not questioned in 1909 by U S attorney, 74 helpful in 1910 investigation, 77 leaves Panama in 1911, 77, quotes father's warnings, 79, letter from Kingston, 85, willing to testify, 85, with father to see T R, 87, confirmation by Dr Embury, 87, his death in Paris, 88
Amaya, Ramon G, 33, 34
American Atlantic and Pacific Canal Co, 2
American Export Lines, 163
American Legion C Z Dept, 6, 132
A N P A, 53
American Society of Civil Engineers, 154, 163, 172, 173
American Trading & Development Company, 25
"Americanization" of canal company attempted, 10, 11
Americas Daily, 124, 125, 128
Anderson, Judge Albert B, 52, 99, 100
Anderson, Omer, 121

# Index

Ann Arbor, 124
Annuity to Panama, Preface, 105, 114, 137
Annulment of treaties, Preface
Anti-American attitudes, Preface, 110, 111, 126, 133
Arango, Jose Augustin, 23, his *"Data for a History,"* 23, removed from U S Library of Congress, 24, he omitted Cromwell's name, 26, unexpurgated text of his *"Data for a History,"* 71, his telltale letter, 84
Arango, Jose Augustin Jr, 71
Arbitration of Crowell's fees, 94, 95
Archives of French, undelivered to U.S, 51, 63
Arias, Arnulfo, 142, 143, 144
Arias, Ricardo, 24, 25, 31, 65, 69
Arias, Ricardo M, 132, 135
Arias, Roberto, 126
Arias, Tomas, 25, 32, 34, 69, 71, 83
d'Armand, R. A, 66
Arosemena, Alcibiades, 144
Arosemena, Carlos C, 25
Arosemena, Pablo, 44
Associated Press, 85
Aspinwall, William H, 2
Atlee, Clement, 124
Atomic bomb problems, 156
Atrato River, 165

## B

Balboa, 1
Baltimore & Ohio bonds, 71
Bankers Trust Company, 59
Bank of North America, 10
Bargaining power of U S. thrown away, Preface, 130
Bates, Lindon W., 102
Beaupre, A M, 19, 21
Beers, George K, 30
Beers, James R, 23, on "delicate mission," 24, 25, 44, 71 sees Cromwell and returns with codes, 24
Belmont, August, 10
"Benefits" for Panama, Preface, 109, 134
Bennett, Ira E, 172
Bigelow, John, 28
Birth certificate of Panama Republic, 145
Black, Major William Murray, 37
Blackmail, charges of, 48
Blackmail, political, 81

"Blackmailers" unidentified, 7, never prosecuted, 49, 50
Black Sea Straits, 122
Bo, Marius, 14
Board of Consultants, 162, 163, 164, 170, 171
Bombardment of Panama City, 34
Bonaparte, Charles J, 51
Bonner, Herbert C, 161, 162, 163
Boston, U S S, 33
Bowling Green Trust Co, 71, 147
Boyd, Aquilino, 134, 135
Boyd, Federico, taken into conspiracy, 25, his house becomes meeting-place, 31, with Amador in New York, 40, one of four who ran the "revolution," 69, swears no more than 50 knew "revolution" was planned, 69
Boyd, Samuel, 35, 79, 84
Braden, Spruille, his Latin American experience, 108, frustrated by Pentagon and State Department, 109, 110
Bradley, Willis W, 155
Bribe money, its source and recipients, 35, 36
Bridge across Canal, 117
Brown, Charles, 64
Brown, Constantine, 6
Brown, Hilton U, 52, 53
Brown, Vernon H, 10, 59
Bryan-Chamorro Treaty, Preface, 167, 168, 169, 170
Buchanan, Kenneth, 113
Bunau-Varilla, Maurice, 15
Bunau-Varilla, Philippe his lobbying, 15, his "chance incident," 28, gets Cromwell re-employed, 14, designated as Minister, 36, received at White House, 39, authority in jeopardy, 38, drafted 1903 treaty, 39, 40, avoided Amador and Boyd, 41, threatened to resign, 42, resigned, 42, forced his own appointment, 90, hated by Panamanians, 146, denies what he said in Paris, 94, what he did say in Paris as recorded by Seitz and Hereford, 90 to 94, denounced Cromwell, 91, contradicts himself, 94, dies in Paris, 146
Bungling and Waste, 152
Bureaucracies unwatched, 152
Burton, Theodore E., 18
Butler, John Marshall, 129
Byrd, Harry Flood, 116

## C

Cables. for U S warships, 32, to discredit Bunau-Varilla, 44, records destroyed, 71, 72
Cabinet of first government, 36
Cadiz to Cathay, 172
Cambridge, Mass , 124
Canal routes, search for, 1
Canal Zone status – by perpetual grant, not by lease, 145
Canal Zone Government, 151, 158
Canal Zone, a wider zone needed, 103
Carmichael, Otto, 97
Case, Francis, 116
Castillero, Ernesto, 134
Central & South American Telegraph Co , 70
Chaco Peace, 108
Chamber of Commerce of Panama, 111
Chanis, Daniel Jr , 143
Chapman, William F Jr , 10
Charlottesville, N C , 68
Chauncey, Henry, 2
Chiari, Roberto F , 143
Christian Science Monitor, 6, 123
CIO 106
Clark, Henry W , 10
Clark University, 47, 102
Cloman, Sidney A (alias S A Otts), 30
Cobb, Frank Irving, 97, 98, 99
Codes, 24, 32, 76 83
Colombia treaty of 1846-48 2, diplomacy manipulated by Cromwell, 16, 17, Constitution, 21 troops at Colon 33, garrison in Panama was paid, 80, supplied suppressed cables, 80
Columbia Club, Indianapolis, 99
Columbia University School of Medicine, 66
Communist influences, Preface, 106, 131, techniques, 131, 138, 151
"Compagnie Du Canal de Panama Company," 58
Comptroller General of U S , 152, 164, 172
Concessions to Panama, 117
Concha, Jose Vicente, 17
Congress of U S , taxpayers look to, 164
Congressional Library, 24
Congressional Record, 111, 122, 157, 173

Constitution of Panama, 101
Consultants, Board of, 162, 163, 164, 170, 171
Contempt, threats of, 54
Converse, E C , 10, 59
Costa Rica, 128, 150, 168
Coverdale & Colpitts, 163
Coverup technique, 85, 89
Coverups of French records, 62, of Panamanian opulence, 89, by Law 48 of 1904, 89, 90
Credit Lyonnais, 31
Crises and confusions, 163
Cromwell, Nelson P , 60
Cromwell, William Nelson retained to divert U S. from Nicaragua to Panama, 4, 7, his methods self-described, 5, 9, defied Senator Morgan, 7, his "vigorous policy," 8, services suspended, 11, re-engaged, 14 15, manipulates Colombian diplomacy, 16, 17, conferences with T R , 19, 20, closeness to Sec Hay, 17, 18 his threat to Colombia, 19, welcomes Amador, 26 warns Panama Railroad employees, 27, 28, pushes Amador out of his office 27, his "brief" confirmed in Paris, 63, text of his "brief" in House hearings 173, at Raoul Amador's Waldorf luncheon, 74, accompanied Taft to Panama, 82, tries to get Bunau-Varilla removed, 90, his fee cut in Paris, 94 95, as Fiscal Agent of Panama 95 his fortune, 95 as Who's Who described him, 147, his death 95
Cullom, Shelby M , 21
Curtis, William J 29, 48, 74
Cutter, Luke H , 66

## D

Darling, Charles Hial, 33
Daughters of the American Revolution, 5, 133
David, 45
"Dear Little Son' letter how discovered, 72, 73, how it escaped destruction, 74
Declaration of Independence, 37
Defense sites agreement, 106, 107
Defense bases rights renounced by U S , 105, U S kicked off, 110, lease extension refused, 110, treaty rejected, 110, 143, U S. withdraws from bases, 110

## Index    177

Delamar, J. R., 10, 58, 59, 60
"Deliberate judgment of the Congress" — how deliberate? 16
Dellay, Vincent J, 133
Deming, S, 74
Democratic National Committee, 48, Platform Committee, 122, national convention, 122
Depew, Chauncey M, 56, 59 60
Diaz, Temistocles, 133, 134, 141
"Disappointed," 84
Discord, endemic, 141
Dixie, U S S, 31, 33
Donations, 15
Dorn, Francis E, 132, 156
Drake, E A, 26, 44, 74
Du Bois, James T, 149, 150
Dulles, John Foster, 120, 122, 148
Dunlap, Harry L, 65
Duque, J Gabriel, 26, 89
Duque, Carlos, 27
DuVal, Miles P, 154, 172

### E

Echeverria, M J, 74
Edgerton, Glen E, 157
Edie, Major Guy L, 30
Edwards, Clarence E, 102
"Egyptianization" of Suez 119
Ehrman, Elmira, 88
Ehrman. Felix, 35, 38
Eisenhower, Dwight D, 120
Eisenhower, Milton S, 120, 139
Elliston, Herbert Berridge, 123
Embury, Dr Philip, 86, 87
Eminent domain, 105
Endicott Hotel, 25
Ervin, Sam J Jr, 116
Espinosa B, Manuel, 25, 69
Espionage, 55, 80
Esprielle, Francisco V de la, 36
Expropriation, Preface, 124

### F

Fabrega, Julio J, 36
Fabrega, Octavio, 112, 126
Facio, Francisco Antonio, 36
Facts that belong to history, Preface
Fairbanks, Charles W, 43
Farnham, Roger L, 8, 20, 26, 35, 40, 65, 74, 85
Farrell, Thomas F, 156
Federal reservations, 53
Fifth Avenue Hotel, 40
Fifty/fifty division, Preface, 114, 126, 134, 135, 139, 140

Financing of "revolution," 25, 35 36, 38, 71, 90, 147, Bunau-Varilla takes all the credit, 29, 30
"First aid de camp," 42
Flag of Panama, 30, 31, made by Mme Bunau-Varilla, 30, raised by U S. Army Major Black, 37, presented to T R, 42
Flag planting in Canal Zone, Preface, 138
Flanders, Ralph E, 121, 122
Flint, Charles R, 10, 25, 59
Flood, Daniel J, Preface, 126, 130, 132, 133, 153, 155, on juridical basis of sovereignty, 132, concurrent resolution, 133, on Panamanian instability 141 to 144
Fontaine, S S, 86
Fort Revere, Mass, 25, 66, 73, 87
Forty million dollars, see "Who got the money"
Founding Fathers, 82, 103
Fournier, Fabio, 126
Freedom of the Press, 4, 96, 99
French arbitrators, their award, 94, 95
French failure at Panama, 4
Friel, Francis S, 163
Frisbee, Admiral, 66
Fuller, Thomas S, 65, 67, 68, 69, 70
Fulbright, J W, 116

### G

Gaitskell, Hugh, 124
Gannett Newspapers, 166
Garay, Narciso, 103
General Staff, orders to, 30
"Geographic resources," 126
Georgetown University, 135
Gibraltar, 110, 127
Giveaway policy of U S started at Panama 104 111
"Giveaway and Get'more," 124
Goethals, George W, 172
Gontard, Paul, 94
Gore, Albert, 116
Gould, George J, 59, 60
Grant, Ulysses S, 2
Gresham, Bertha Kennard, 66, 67, 87
Gresham, Lt, William, U S N, 66
Gridiron Club, 97
Groves, Gen. Leslie R, 162
Guardia, Ernesto de la Jr, 132, 134, 139
Guardia, Ricardo Adolfo de la, 142

Guizado, Jose Ramon 132, 144
Guyol, Edwin Warren, 79

## H

Hahn, Capt. William G, alias Howard, 30
Hains, Col Peter C., 9
Hall, Henry N, 76
Hammond, John Craig, 55, 56, 57, 59
Hanna, Mark, 14, 15, 18, 43
Hanna Minority Report, 16
Harriman, E H, 48, 56
Haupt, Lewis M, 9, 12, 13, 14
Hay, John, 26, 29, 39
Hayes, Rutherford B, 2
Hay-Bunau-Varilla Treaty contrasted with Hay-Herran, 39, secretly signed at Hay's home, 41, ratified by Panama, 42, hated by Panamanians, 147
Hay-Herran Treaty initiated and drafted by Cromwell, 17, 18, ratified by U S Senate, 19, rejected by Colombia, 21, now longed-for by Panama, 135
Hay-Pauncefote Treaty, 3
Hearst Newspapers, 166, 167, 168
Hearst, William Randolph, 166, 167
Hebard, R W, 172
Heidelbach, Ickelheimer & Co, 31
Hepburn Bill, 14, 15
Hereford, William R, 91, 92, 93
"Hero of the Republic," 65
Herran, Tomas, 17, 27
Heurtematte, Roberto M, 112
Havana, 78
"Hijo Benemerito," 82
Hill, Edward Bruce, 61, 67, 70, 74
Hill, Edward J, 59
Hill, J R, 60, 61
Hines, Frank T, 108
Hiss, Alger, 109, 111, 112, 130
History of Panama gaps filled in, Preface, unknown to this generation, Preface, clouded by contradictions, 146
"Hold-up" charges false, 20, 21
Hollister, S C, 162
"Hopes," 84
Hotel Central, 77, 82
Hough, Judge Charles M, 64, 97
"Hound's tooth, as clean as," 70
Howard, H E, 30
Hubbard, John, 34
Huertas, Esteban, 34, 35, 80
Hull, Cordell, 103

Humphrey, Capt. C B., 30
Humphrey, Hubert H., 122
Hutin, Maurice, 64

## I

Independence Day, 33
Independence of Panama no longer guaranteed by U S, 104
Indianapolis News, Preface, 50, 51, 52, 99
Indianapolis Press Club, 53
Instability of Panama government, 101, 165 to 170
Interamerican Conference of 1956, 120
International Conference on Interoceanic Canals, 125
International law, 125
Internationalization of Panama Canal, Preface, 112, 119, 121, 122, 123, 124, 150
Interoceanic Canals Commission projected, 161
Isthmian Canal Commission, 51
Isthmian Canal Policy, 163, 172
Ivins, William M, 11

## J

Jackson, Henry M, 116
Jeffries, F L, 60
Jeffries, Herbert Ottley, 36, 60, 80
Jerome, William Travers, 48
Jimenez, Enrique A, 108, 109, 142
Johnston, Ohn D, 116
Journal of Race Development, 102
Juliao, Victor N, 138, 139
Junta of Government, 34
Juridical basis of Canal Zone, 132

## K

Kahn, Otto H, 61
Kealing, Joseph B, 51
Kennard, William Edward, 66
Kerr, Robert S., 116
Kiel Canal, 122
Kingston, Jamaica, 24, 31, 33, 79
Kittredge, A B, 18, 43
Klein, Julius, 113
Knapp, James R, 67, 70
Knowland, William F, 168
Kuhn, Loeb & Co, 10, 48, 61

## L

Labor unions move in, 106
"Labor's Good Neighbor Policy," 106

*Index* 179

Lake Nicaragua, 2, 170
Laffan, William, 50
Lalley, Joseph M , 173
La Nacion, 141
Latin American Conference of 1913, 47, 102
Latin American distrust of U S , one cause of, 149
Law 48 of 1904, 89, 90
LeFevre, Ernesto, 83
Legion Magazine, 6
Le Matin, 28
Leon, Maurice, 63
Lesseps, Ferdinand d, 15
Libel charges by T R indictments in Washington, 51, in New York, 53, first defeat in Indianapolis, 52, tried in New York, 97, dismissed by U S Supreme Court, 98
Lindo, Joshua, 25, 83
Lindsay, John D , 65
Lobbying, 3, 8, 158
Lombardo Toledano, Vicente, 106
London Times, 126
Long, Russell B , 116
Loomis, Francis B , 29, 32, 36, 92
Los Angeles Examiner, 167, 168
Louisiana Purchase, Preface
Lyman, Robert Hunt, 51, 99

**M**

McCann, William R., 159
McClellan, George B , 35
McKinley, William, 9
McNamara, Stuart, 51, 54, 58, 64
Mackay, Clarence, 59, 60
Magnuson, Warren G , 116
Makeshift, 152, 153
Mansfield, Michael J , 128, 129
Marblehead, U S S , 33
Marine operating problems, 154, 172
Maritime Canal Company of Nicaragua, 3
Marshall Plan, 104
Martin, Thomas E , 132, 156, 157
Melendez, Porfirio, 35
"Memorandum of Agreement," 11, 12, 58
Mendoza, Carlos A , 36
Merchant Marine Committee, 133, 161
Methodist Reporter, 127, 128
Mexican War, effect on Canal, 2
Meyer, Eugene, 123
Miller, Warner, 3
Miner, Dwight C , 173

Miraflores locks, 153
Modernization plans and progress, 160, 161
Monopoly at Panama, alternative to, 165
Montgomery, Ruth, 6
Moore, John Bassett, 148
Morales, Eusebio A , 36, 80
Moreno, Miguel J , 135, 136
Morgan, J P & Co , 10, 59, 60, 62, 71
Morgan, John T , 8, 47, 58, 60, 85
Morrow, J J , 153
Morton, Levi P , 10
Mountains Will Move, 172
Murray, Philip, 106
Murphy, Grayson Mallet-Prevost, 30
Murrow, Edward R , 124

**N**

"Napoleonic strategy," 8
Nashville, Tenn , 127
Nashville, U S S , 31, 32, 33, 34
Nassau Bank, 56
Nasser, Preface, 120, 124
National Economic Council, 111
National Rivers & Harbors Congress, 158
National Tube Company, 10, 59
Nationalization of Canal by Panama, Preface, 119, 140, 150
Navigational problems of Canal, 154
Navy, U S , orders, 32, 33
Neuberger, Richard L , 116
New Granada, 2
New York Central Railroad, 56
New York Herald, 21, 35, 85
New York Journal, 66
New York Sun, 50
New York Times, 10, 121, 122, 165
New York Tribune, 10
New York World, Preface, 10 48, 50
Newsweek, 115
Nicaragua Canal, Preface, 150, 162, 165, 167, 168, 169, 170, 171
Nicaragua Canal Construction Co., 3
Nicaraguan Strait Development Co , Inc , 170
Nicoll, De Lancey, 97
Nixon, Richard M , Preface, 139
North American Newspaper Alliance, 121, 123
North American Review, 81

## O

Obaldia, Jose Domingo de, 60, 81
Obarrio, Nicanor A de, 25, 36
Obsolescence of Panama Canal, 162
"Occupied territory" 130
"Operation Sovereignty," Preface. 137
Oppenheim, Eugene, 11
Oregon, voyage of the 3
Organization of American States, 120
Ossa, Francisco de la, 76, 77
Otts, S A , 30
Outlook Magazine 99

## P

Paine, Charles 74
Panama Canal Company of America (Cromwell's), 10, 11
Panama Canal Company (U S Gov't) new organization and functions, 151 158 operating figures and problems 160, 161 demand for its liquidation, 140
Panama Canal Societies in five cities 159
Panama Canal U S control at stake, Preface U S sovereignty challenged, Preface, importance of, Preface, 6, dangers that threaten it, 5, who have been alerted, 5, 6
Panama funds, 64
Panama Journal, 84
Panama lottery, 26
Panama Obligation Pool Account, 61
Panama Railroad the first transcontinental, 2, 172, sold to the French, 4, employees responsible to Cromwell, 23, its funds used to bribe Colombian soldiers 35, 89, terminals given to Panama, 117, abandonment blocked by U S Congress, 117
"Panama scandal," 7, 48, 54, 96
Panama Star & Herald, 26 89, 115
Pan American Society of U S , 113
Panic of 1893 stopped canal financing, 3
Pavey, Frank D , 40, 91, 92
Pearson, Drew, 122, 123
Pedromiguel bottleneck, 153
Penalized stockholders, 4, 15
Perkins, George W , 60
Permission vs right, 104

Perpetuity of Canal Zone grant: limitation rejected, 115, abrogation demanded, 126, 140
Phi Delta Theta 53
Pollak, Francis D , 10
Population of Panama, 1903 and 1958, 144
Potsdam Conference, 122, 123
Potter, Gov. William E , 160, 162
Prague, source of propaganda, 120, 121
Prescott. Herbert G   23, 25, 30, 32, 33, 42, 78
Prescott Richard 33
Press Publishing Co , 53
Pressure on witnesses, 70
Principals of 'revolution' only four, 69
Propaganda, pro-Panama, anti-Nicaragua, 8
Provisional Government, 36
Publicity feared and valued by Cromwell, 48
Publicity, vigorous policy by Cromwell 8
Public order – left to Panamanians 105
Pulitzer, Joseph, Preface, indicted 51, opposed compromise, 97, vindicated, 99

## Q

Quintanilla, Luis, 120
Quintero, Cesar, 126

## R

Radical ideologies, 103
Rainey, Henry T  91, 173
Randolph, E  Sydney, 156, 157, 162
Records of New York World, preserved, 58, of the French, sealed, 62
Reforms at Canal grow slowly, 151, ordered by Congress, 151
Remon, Jose Antonio, 109, 112, 113, 114, 115, 144
Rental paid for defense sites, 108
Reporter Magazine, 122
Republic of the Isthmus, 31, 34, 36
Republican Party, 11, 48, 81, campaign contribution by Cromwell, 94
Revolt, armed, in 1945, 142, 143

# Index

"Revolution" of 1903 exact date foretold, 20, knowledge of limited to 50, 69, as originally planned, 31, total casualties, 78, whole truth never told, 79, veil of deceit 84, revolt in 1931, 142
Reyes, Rafael, 44, 45
Rhine-Danube Canal, 122
Rights vs permission, 104
Ries, Maurice, 6
Rio Hato air base, 107, 108, 109, 117, 118
Riots, 138, 142
Roberts, Edward J., 64
Robertson, Willis A., 116
Robinson, Douglas, 11, 49, 58, 59, 60, 61, 64
Roderick George H., 157
Roeder, Gus C., 65
Rogatory commissions, 62, testimony in Panama re-read 70 Panama witnesses concealed, 80
Rogers H H, 58, 59
Roosevelt, Franklin D, 102 103 154
Roosevelt, James, 124
Roosevelt Theodore (T R) Preface, 47, 50, 52 54, 55 97, "I took the Isthmus," 81, 100, "I have nothing to say!" 100
Roosevelt, Quentin, 100
Rowe E. Hartley, 162
Russell Richard B, 116

## S

Saenz, Vicente, 126
Ste Croix, Alexander de, 79
Salinas Bay, 170
San Blas Indians, 45
"Sanctified territory," 38
Sands, William F, 173
Sangree, Allen, 48
Satterlee, H J, 60
Saturday Evening Post, 6
Schiff, Jacob H, 61
Sea-level at Panama, Preface, would require new treaty, 158, cost and effect on tolls, 157, 158, plan ignored by Congress, 158, should it be undertaken? 163
Security of Panama Canal, Preface, 154, 155
Seitz, Don C, 56, 67, 91
Seligman, Isaac, 58, 59, 60
Seligman, J. & W, 10, 58, 61
Seybold, John S, 151

Shaler, James R., 23, 27, 33, "Hero of the Republic," 65
Sibert, William L, 154, 173
Simmons, J Edward, 10, 14, 58, 59, 60
Skinner, Ralph, 6
Slater, John E, 162
Smith, Delavan, 50, 51, 97
Smith, Lawrence H, 111
Social workers, 114
Somoza, Anastasio, 165
Sovereignty Claims by Panamanians Preface, 109, 119, as drafted by Bunau-Varilla, 39, as stated in Colombian treaty, 39, 40, dual sovereignty breeds friction, 10, 102, titular, as claimed, 132, 134, Panamanian demands renewed, 138, 139, U S sovereignty perpetual, 145
Spain 3
Spanish language, Preface 139, 140
Speculation in French securities, 11 57, 62, profits from 64
Spenders' lobbies and methods, 160
Sperry Rand Corp, 162
"Spontaneous uprising,' 35
"Spontaneous' raids, 137
Spooner Bill, 16, passed by margin of five votes 16, by whom inspired and drafted, 94
Squandermania, 152, 153
Stennis, John, 116
Stephens, John L, 2
Stetson, Francis Lynde, 10
Stevens, John F 153, 154, 173
Stevens, John F Jr, 159
Stillman, James, 58, 59
Story of Panama, Congressional hearings, 173
Stratton, James H, 173
Sucre, Carlos, 112
Students 124, 134, 137, 138, 141 second congress of, 134, their ultimatum, 135, strikes, 138, rioting casualties, 138
Suez Canal, Preface, 119 122
Sullivan, Algernon Sydney, 48
Sullivan, George H, 74
Supreme Court, U S, 98, 99
Svarverud, Carl, 170, 171
Syndicate agreement, 58
Syndicate operations, 49, denied by Cromwell, 49, evidence of, 55, 56

## T

Taft agreement of 1904, 101
Taft, Charles P., 49
Taft, Henry W., 49, 58, 59, 60, 61
Taft, William Howard, 47, 53, 82, 93
Tascon, Leoncio, 34
Technical cooperation from U S, 114
Tehauntepec, 165
Teheran, 104
Teran, Oscar 70, 77, 81
Terminal Lake-Third Locks Plan, Preface, 154, 155, 163
Terminal cities, Panama and Colon, 31, 102
Thatcher, Maurice H , 159, 160
Third locks fiasco, 153
Thompson, Clark W., 132, 158, 173
Thompson-Urrutia Treaty, 149
Thurmond, Strom, 116
Timberland concession, 65
Tivoli Hotel, 68, 77
Tomlinson, Edward, 6
Torres, Eliseo, 34, 36
Tovar, Juan B., 33, 34
"Tragedy of errors," 146
Transfer fee, 17, 18, 21, 148
Treaties Hay-Bunau-Varilla, demands for changing, 102, 111, 163, 1936-39 Treaty signed and ratified, 103, its impact, 103 104 1955 Treaty, signed and ratified, 115, inadequately debated, 116, fourteen Senators who opposed, 116, concessions to Panama, 117, token return to U S , 117, 118, Memorandum of Understandings, 116
Truman, Harry S , 122, 123

## U

Ultimatum to Colombia, 19, 20
Union Pacific bonds, 71
United Fruit Company, 162
United Nations, Panama at, 109, 130, 134, 135, 136, 143
United Press, 122, 125, 126, 128
University of California, 100
University of Panama, 134
U S. Naval Institute, 172

## V

Valdes, Hector, 69, 70
Vanderbilt, Cornelius, 2
Van Hamm, Caleb M., 49, 51, 53, 99
Van Norden, Warner, 10
Van Voorhis, Daniel, 107
Volcano propaganda by Buneau-Varilla and Cromwell, 15, 94

## W

Waldorf-Astoria, 29, 74
Walker, John G , 9, 12
Walker, William, 2
Walker Commissions, 9, 10, 12, 15
Walker, R. L., 74
Wallace, John F , 78, 93
Warburg, James P., 62, 121, 122
Warburg, Paul M., 62
Washington Evening Star, 121, 132
Washington Post, 122, 123
Welles, Sumner, 103
West Point, 53
White House, visits to by Bunau-Varilla, 29, by Amador, 85, 86, 87
Whitley, Jonas M , 8, 44, 49, 65
"Who got the money?" 5, 46, 50, 60
Williams, Charles R , 51, 99
Windsor Trust Co , 59
Winslow, Lanier & Co , 59, 60
Wise, Henry A., 64
World's Work, 102
Wright, Luke, 51
"Wrongs against Panama" refuted, 43, 80

## Y

Yalta, 104
"Yanqui aggression," 107
Yavisa, 44
Young, G W., 60
Youth, Panamanian their permanent aspiration, Preface, they do not know their country's history, 103, 145

## Z

Zenger, John Peter, Preface, 99
Zihacus, 110

CPSIA information can be obtained
at www.ICGtesting.com
Printed in the USA
LVHW051352220621
690858LV00007B/229